Introducing EMOTIONAL INTELLIGENCE

MASTERY THE MODERN PSYCHOLOGY TO CONTROL EMOTIONS, IMPROVE COMMUNICATION AND BOOST YOUR LEADERSHIP SKILLS

By

Daniel Anderson

COPYRIGHT © 2019. ALL RIGHTS RESERVED.

No part of this publication may be reproduced, distributed, or transmitted in any form or by any means, including photocopying, recording, or other electronic or mechanical methods, or by any information storage and retrieval system without the prior written permission of the publisher, except in the case of very brief quotations embodied in critical reviews and certain other noncommercial uses permitted by copyright law.

TABLE OF CONTENTS

INTRODUCTION 5
EMOTIONAL INTELLIGENCE 15
EMOTION AND INTELLIGENCE 29
CRUSHING STRESS WITH EMOTIONAL INTELLIGENCE 34
ROLE OF EMPATHY IN LIFE 40
EMOTIONAL MATURITY AND EMOTIONAL INTELLIGENCE 43
FUNDAMENTALS OF EMOTIONAL INTELLIGENCE 48
EMPATHY VS EMOTIONAL INTELLIGENCE 53
WHY IS EMOTIONAL INTELLIGENCE IMPORTANT? 58
IMPROVING YOUR LEVEL OF EMOTIONAL INTELLIGENCE 63
TYPES OF EMOTIONAL INTELLIGENCE 68
BENEFIT OF EMOTIONAL INTELLIGENCE 73
EMOTIONAL INTELLIGENCE FOR LEADERS 81
LEADERSHIP LIFESTYLE TO EMULATE 99
LOW EMOTIONAL CAPABILITIES CAN RUIN YOU 107
EI FOR THE SALESMAN 110

12 ELEMENTS OF EMOTIONAL INTELLIGENCE 120

EMOTIONAL INTELLIGENCE IN THE HOME: RAISING EMOTIONALLY INTELLIGENT CHILDREN 123

UNDERSTANDING THE EMOTIONS OF OTHERS 128

EMOTIONAL INTELLIGENCE AND SELF-ESTEEM 133

HOW TO USE THE ABCDE THEORY OF EMOTIONS 140

MASTERY OF EMOTION: A KEY TO A BETTER LIFE 145

GROWING EMOTIONAL INTELLIGENCE 149

CONCLUSION 162

INTRODUCTION

Emotional intelligence has a lot to do with being intelligent, and intelligence is a skill that can be developed upon, man is an emotional being and emotional beings are individuals with feelings, complex feelings as a result of the many happenings that occur on day to day basis can create various issues for humans and how they relate with people, emotional intelligence helps individuals come to grip with this inborn ability that we have been created with and helps us to understand humans around us. Through empathy people can place themselves in the experiences of others and understand how they are feeling. Using skills like self-awareness, self-motivation individuals can improve on their emotional illiteracy and be more aware of themselves, to attain mastery of emotions you would need to take cognizance of your character. Emotional intelligent people are great masters of emotions, they are individuals who are masters at communication, leading teams and learning from mistakes, they are not selfish and through the course of this book we would take time to explain how to achieve emotional intelligence for leaders, at the workplace and at the home how parents can raise emotional children. We would come to understand that lack of adequate emotional intelligence can be a barrier to growth and the attainment of success.

We use our emotions to control how we react to situations and is therefore a major factor in determining our personality, who we are. The number of definitions as to what emotional intelligence really is are, of course, far too many and complex for this short article however, what we can confirm is that there are two constants in all this. Firstly, the concept of what emotions are and secondly, understanding the context of emotions.

Today we can clearly see that being only "book smart" and having a high intelligence quotient or IQ does not guarantee a successful, happy and fulfilled life. There are many people in all parts of the world who are very brilliant academically but are inept at dealing with people and successful at work or in their personal relationships. Academic intelligence is not enough on its own to be successful in life. IQ can help you get a job and earn a living, but it does not show you how to live a life. When it comes to happiness and success in life, emotional intelligence helps you build stronger relationships, succeed at work, and achieve your career and personal goals.

Emotionally intelligent people are able to recognize their own emotional state and the emotional states of others and as a result they connect more easily with people. They therefore communicate better, form stronger relationships, achieve greater success at work, and lead a more fulfilling life. John Gottman was right when he said "In the last decade or so, science has discovered a tremendous amount about the role emotions play in our lives. Researchers have found that even more than IQ, your emotional awareness and abilities to handle feelings will determine your success and happiness in all walks of life, including family relationships."

Our natural state of being, as one with Soul, is a harmonious state of Love, in which the only feelings are of continuous peace and bliss. Therefore if we are feeling any feeling other than peace and bliss, we have got out of balance somewhere. This is due to our conditioned and faulty thinking, which emerges as tolerations, needs and limiting beliefs. Using our Emotional Intelligence equips us to identify the message that Soul is sending us through these feelings, so we can rectify our thinking and thus move always towards Love.

Being Emotionally Intelligent is my ability to consciously comprehend my own emotional States of Being. Being 'Emotional' means that I am aware of the feeling that is my emotional state of being. Being 'Intelligent' means I have a rational knowledge or logical understanding of the situation, occurrence and circumstances that I am currently experiencing. I am

Intelligent when I can consciously rationalize what is happening in my reality. I am Emotional when I can feel the awareness of my energetic state of being - my emotional energy.

Emotional Intelligence loses clarity when I confuse 'being emotional' with 'being irrational'. When I am studying negative states of being that cause me to subconsciously react, I am learning about my own irrational behavior that is without emotional intelligence. I am studying 'irrational intelligence'.

Being emotional is not reacting irrationally; it is being consciously-aware of my emotional state of being. I never react emotionally because with emotional intelligence I am always able to respond intelligently. Negative emotional states of being are irrational because a rationally intelligent person who is emotionally aware (intelligent) would never choose to experience them. Understanding irrational behavior does require emotional intelligence but it is not the definition of Emotional Intelligence. The true test of my Emotional Intelligence is whether I can be Happy & Well as a result of my conscious choice to be so. It is only my emotional ignorance that is depriving me of the happiness and well-being that is my true nature.

Happiness is an emotional feeling. How can a rational man be happy in a state of being disconnected and unemotional? Well-being is an emotional feeling. How can I feel well in a society that medicates physical and mental illness without one iota of emotional intelligence?

Having sympathy for other people doesn't mean anything unless I have defined the compassion that I am feeling. Defining compassion as: "Wanting to relieve the suffering of others", is a rationally intelligent definition of a physical desire not the explanation of an emotional feeling.

It is my lack of emotional intelligence that disconnects me from my true emotional nature. A analytical world has become a world that is devoid of lasting and Happiness, and a world filled with sadness and sickness. We seem to have lost our connection to our true Wealth and our true Health when, as a society, we are divided from our Emotional Intelligence.

Emotional States Of Being

Professional on the study of emotions have claimed that about 90% of emotional information that we feel is transmitted through non verbal means, by tone, gesture and glance and that we are rarely consciously awake of how much we are transmitting or reading from others.

To have to deny, to lie about, to suppress feelings, or to be blind to the feelings of others causes tensions and anxieties that limit us in our ability to connect to and live with others. It is needful that we develop emotional intelligence because the ability to move easily and interact freely in the emotional world is a very important part of what it requires to live an true and happy life on earth.

Emotional 'States of Being' require definition before I can understand them intelligently. When I define an emotional state of being, I give it definition, it becomes a definite emotion, and I become consciously-aware of its existence.

It is my conscious-awareness of the definite nature of my emotions that allows me to be emotionally intelligent.

An 'Emotional' person is aware of their feelings as different emotions.

An 'Emotionally Intelligent' person is a person who is able to consciously define their emotional state of being and create it at will, if and when they so choose. By intelligently defining an emotion, I become both emotionally aware of the feeling and rationally conscious of its definition. I cannot experience a definite emotion unless I am able to define it accurately. In the absence of naming an emotion, it will remain either a positive or a negative experience, dependent on the beliefs that I hold in my sub-conscious.

I have defined emotion (emotional state of being) with an adjective, which is a describing word. Any adjective that describes my feelings or my emotional state of being is an emotion. Without an adjective to describe it and name the expression, an emotion is just a feeling that is really hard to understand. One should not feel that Being emotional is reacting irrationally; it is being mentally-aware of my emotional state of being. I never react emotionally because with emotional intelligence I know how to respond intelligently during situations that call for response. Negative emotional states of being are irrational because a rationally intelligent person who is emotionally conscious (intelligent) would not choose to experience them, they are just not good for you. Understanding irrational behaviour does require emotional intelligence but it is not the definition of Emotional Intelligence.

The Potential Of My Emotional Energy

Emotion is an energetic state of being that I am experiencing. All forms of energy have a force, a magnitude and a potential. Emotions are no different. The potential of any energy is realized when the force and magnitude of that energy unite.

Electrical energy has a force called 'volts', a magnitude called 'amps' and a potential called 'watts'. They are all named after the person who first defined them. Emotional energy is more complicated because not only is its potential divided by force and magnitude but its force is divided by polarity and its magnitude is divided by gender.

The polarity of my emotions is either positive or negative and the gender of my energy is either male or female. (Anger & pride are male whereas meekness & humility are female. However, Impatience and intolerance are usually seen as negative and patience and tolerance as positive).

The degree, to which my emotional energy is unbalanced, by being divided by either polarity or gender or both, determines the intensity of the emotion that I am feeling. The greater is the imbalance the greater is the intensity of the emotional feeling. The intensity of my emotional state of being is the product of both the gender and the polarity of the emotional energy.

Emotional Intelligence requires not only the definition of my emotional state of being but the understanding of its potential for my Life.

Understanding the potential of my emotional energy requires me to be consciously-aware of:

- ✓ Its force and magnitude
- ✓ Its gender, polarity and intensity

✓ Its definition or Adjectivity

✓ The sponsoring thought or thoughts that are creating the emotion.

The Ultimate Potential of my Emotional Energy is the Pure Feeling of Love that emanates from my Soul.

Life is an emotional experience.

My Emotional Intelligence requires more than my ability to manage my irrational behavior. It requires the ability to understand my emotional experiences intelligently. The cause of my irrational behavior is my lack of emotional intelligence. I react irrationally with what is sometimes confusingly called an emotional reaction.

I respond with positive emotion once I attain the intelligence and understanding to do so. My symptoms of irrational behavior are created by my lack of rational intelligence. Extreme irrational behavior caused by a lack of rational ability may be diagnosed as a mental illness by a rational person who has no emotional intelligence.

Diagnosing emotional disorder or disease requires emotional intelligence not rational intelligence, which is probably why illness is usually diagnosed as either physical or mental and not emotional. In the absence of emotional intelligence, my life became an unemotional experience as a rationally intelligent man.

In a dualistic world, the more rationally intelligent I become the more contained, disconnected and emotionally unintelligent I am. It is my experience that the more I rationalize my world with tolerance and patience the less I react with the frustration of my anger and intolerance. However, with emotional intelligence I consciously choose to be 'Accepting' instead of tolerant and I choose to be 'Allowing' instead of patient. I no longer choose to be a tolerant patient who is patiently tolerating Life.

I have decided to accept that Life as an emotional experience because I am learning to be emotionally intelligent enough to see it that way.

EMOTIONAL INTELLIGENCE

Emotional intelligence which stands for EI, is the unlearned attribute humans have to detect, assess, and affect their own emotion and the emotions of other people in their immediate environment. This concept of emotional intelligence itself started with Dr. Wayne Payne in the year 1985, but emotional intelligence became popular when the author Daniel Goldman came up with a book on Emotional Intelligence , EI also refers to the an individual's ability to identify and manage one's own emotions, as well as the emotions of others. Though there is some disagreement within the circle of psychologists as to what constitutes true emotional intelligence, it is generally said to include at least three skills: emotional awareness, or the ability to identify and name one's own emotions; the ability to harness those emotions and apply them to tasks like thinking and problem solving; and the ability to manage emotions, which includes both regulating one's own emotions when necessary and cheering up or calming down other people.

Emotional intelligence can also be defined as that in born natural ability to recognize and understand emotions in yourself and others, and your ability to use this knowledge to manage your person, relationships and relationships around you. Emotional intelligence is the "something" in each of us that is a bit abstract. It affects how we manage behavior, how we meander through social complexities, and make individual decisions in one's life so as to achieve positive results in life's endeavors. This ability called emotional intelligence taps into a key element of human behavior that is distinct from your intellect. There is no known connection between IQ and EQ; you simply can't predict EQ based on how smart someone is. Cognitive intelligence, or IQ, is not flexible. Your IQ except in the case of traumatic event such as a brain injury remains the same from birth. You don't get smarter by learning new facts or information. Intelligence is your ability to learn, and it's the same at age 10 as it is at age 40. EQ, on the other hand, is a flexible skill that can be groomed. While it is true that some people are naturally more emotionally intelligent than others, a high EQ can be improved upon even if you aren't born with it.

There is currently no validated measurement or scale for emotional intelligence as there is for "g," the general intelligence factor, a fact that has led some critics to claim the concept is either a myth or entirely non-existent. Despite this criticism, however, emotional intelligence (or "emotional quotient," as its sometimes known) has wide appeal among the general public, as well as in certain industries. In recent years, some employers have even incorporated "emotional intelligence tests" into their application or interview processes, on the theory that someone high in emotional intelligence would make a better leader or coworker. But while some studies have found a link between emotional intelligence and job performance, others have shown no correlation, and the lack of a scientifically valid scale makes it difficult to truly measure or predict someone's emotional intelligence on the job.

Identifying individuals who have high EQ is usually very easy. They are very self-aware people and they take their time to reflect on their actions and emotions. They recognize what triggers certain emotions and how to handle them even under desperate circumstances. They also know when they may have reached a "boiling point" and need to cool down or take some steam off the situation for a while; they evaluate the situation of things and come up a solution. It is like hitting the pause button on a remote control.

Studies in the early 1990's by John Mayer and Peter Salovey came up with a working model of emotional intelligence that defined it as the capacity to understand and to reason with emotions. In their analysis, Mayer and Salovey, broke emotional intelligence down into four parts:

Self-Awareness: this is the ability and need to

understand your own emotions, knowing what those emotions are, and acknowledging those feelings. Self-empathy is the act of giving ourselves empathy, listening to our own feelings and unmet needs with compassion and understanding. This does not make the problems go away, or magically make all our needs met. But it does help us to feel connected and centered within ourselves. It can also be a tool to express ourselves with more honesty. Though it doesn't make problems go away, it makes it easier to endure them. It is that natural ability to know which emotions you are experiencing and the reason why you feel that way. When you understand your emotions, it is easier for you to understand, accept and control your emotions and avoid your feelings from controling you. You also become more confident, and bold as you do not let your emotions get out of control. Being self-aware also enables you to take an sincere stance at yourself, be honest with yourself so you can improve on your strengths and know what your weaknesses are, and work on these areas to achieve better outcomes for yourself and others.

You can start to look at Self-Awareness as setting the starting point for your life. For that reason, it is as an essential starting place from which you build the other important aspects of your life. Although Self-Awareness embraces many things, being concious of your own emotions and feelings should be the first and most vital step to take to becoming Emotionally Intelligent. We undergo many different feelings and emotions on a daily basis. These two words (feelings and emotions) are sometimes used interchangeably, but they have different meanings. If we understand the differences, it can greatly shape us into becoming more self-aware about ourselves.

Self-awareness is the foundational competency of the Emotional Intelligence (EI) model and I have made researches and worked on this topic for more than a decade now. This competency provides a solid base upon which to build and enhance Emotional Intelligence competencies including emotional self-management, emotional self-motivation, and empathy and nurturing relationships. Yet many of us go through our day unaware and very accepting of the emotional roller coaster daily events evoke. Without recognizing where we are expanding our emotional energy, it has now become very hard to progress to developing other EI abilities.

Self-Motivation: this is the ability to remain focused on a goal despite your level of self-doubt and impulsiveness. It means feeling physically along with the other person as though their emotions are contagious. It makes one well-attuned to another's emotional world, which is a plus in any of the wide range of callings. There is a downside attached to emotional empathy that occurs, when people lack the ability to manage their own emotions. This can be seen as psychological exhaustion leading to a burnout as commonly seen in professionals. The purposeful detachment cultivated by those in medical profession is a way to void burnout. But when the detachment leads to indifference, it can seriously hamper the professional care.

Individuals who are self-motivated are always eager to take on difficult tasks and challenges, they are self-assured people and are very energetic internally, they are also very good at raising thier voice towards unpopular opinions, they are decisive and resilient.

Empathy: the ability to tune into the feelings of others and effectively understanding them pretty much the same way as they understand themselves. A type of empathy called Cognitive empathy that is the ability to handle emotions in a mature way that is relevant to the present situation. It means knowing how the other person feels and what they might be thinking. It is very helpful in negotiations or motivating people. It has been found that people who possess good cognitive empathy (also called perspective taking) make good leaders or managers because they are able to move people to give their best efforts. But there can be a downside to this type of empathy. If people, falling within the "Dark Triad" - narcissists, Machiavellians and psychopaths - possess ample ability of cognitive empathy, they can exploit others to the extent of torturing them. Such people have no sympathy for their victims and expertly use their ability to carry out their cruelty.

Empathy is very present in humans to many degrees of extents and, therefore, we are affected by the other person's predicament in a different way. In fact, it is one of the first traits of humans so much so that any individual lacking of this ability is seen as not ok, seen as mentally ill or dangerous. From tests carried out and observation Females most times score higher on standard tests of empathy, social sensitivity, and emotion recognition than do males. Its inherence in humans can be proven by the fact that young children respond to the emotions of family members even from that early age, this is proof that its an innate ability. Besides kids, Some domestic animals have also express their worry, when the family members are in distress. There has been reports of dogs rescuing injured persons from fire or detecting sadness. Some pets would stay around and place their heads in their owners' laps , making sounds, and this shows that even animals have empathy. Besides humans, many other species exhibit presence of empathy to a varying extent. Like dolphins who have rescued people on countless occasions and saved people from shark attacks.

A good case scenario for validating the presence of empathy in animals came from these research. The researchers reported in 1964 in the American Journal of Psychiatry that Rhesus monkeys refused to pull a chain that dispatched food to themselves if doing so gave a shock to a companion.one of the monkies stopped pulling the chain for 12 days after witnessing another monkey receive a shock. These primates were literally starving themselves in order to avoid causing harm to one another. We can express empathy through statements such as, "I can see you not very comfortable with this and it doesnt sit well with you," and "I can can see why you are very upset about this issue." We can show empathy through a hug, a pat on the back, body contact, a touch, and even through a "high five to boost morale" when our empathy relates to someone's success. Empathy is not the same emotion as sympathy. Where empathy allows us to vicariously experience and identify with other's feelings, sympathy is a feeling of pity or sorrow for the feelings of others. With empathy we feel with someone else, with sympathy we feel for someone else.

There are many theories concerning the nature versus nurture aspect of empathic development. Are some people born virtuous and some people born evil? Dr. Paul Zak has studied the biological basis of good versus evil behavior over a number of years and has made a very interesting discovery. He found that when people feel for other people, the stress triggers the brain to release a chemical called oxytocin. Likewise, a study at Berkely concluded that a particular variant of the oxytocin receptor gene is associated with the trait of human empathy. In the study, those who had this gene variant were found to have a more empathic nature. Dr. Zak says that this study demonstrates that some people, about five percent of our population, may have a gene variant that makes them less empathic. In other words, he says, some people are more or less immune to oxytocin.

So there is scientific evidence that the goodness trait is encoded in our genes. But nature is not the only influencing factor. We may be born with the capacity to have empathy, but our ability to apply it, to care and understand, is a learned behavior.

Social psychologists say that empathetic behavior is built from the secure attachment babies develop with their parents or primary caregivers, and by modeling their parents' empathetic behavior towards them and others. Sincere empathetic behavior develops in children whose parents constantly show, teach, and reinforce it. It is a gradual emergence that occurs with the consistency and caring shown to them during the formative years of their social and emotional development. In many cases, but not all, adults who lack empathy have been victims of childhood abuse or neglect.

Those who have had extremely painful childhoods, ones that have involved emotional, sexual, or physical abuse, often lose touch with their own feelings while shutting themselves off from the pain. Their underdeveloped coping skills leave them saddled with distress, whether their own or others, and their lack of ability to experience their own pain prevents them from feeling the pain of others. As adults their elaborately built defense mechanisms block guilt and shame while also blocking their conscience. They live life through fear, threats, punishment, and isolation rather than empathy and kindness.

In many cases the opposite is true-the person over-identifies with others' pain, is overwhelmed by it, and becomes overly empathetic to the point that they absorb the feelings of everyone around them. Their internal pain and suffering is triggered when they see others in pain and suffering, therefore become preoccupied with everyone else's pain and make it their own. I did that for most of my life. Often it was to deflect my own pain but ironically it caused me to suffer more. I had very poor coping skills and my boundaries were out of whack if existent at all. I also modeled the behavior I observed as a child.

I do think that overall, my generation, a generation that relied on human interaction, a generation where families visited relatives and friends every Sunday because there was nothing else to do, is more empathetic than the generations that have followed.

In fact, an eye opening new study presented by University of Michigan researchers at an Association for psychological science annual meeting claims that college students who started school after the year 2000 have empathy levels that are 40% lower than students thirty years prior. The sharpest drop occurred in the last nine years. The study includes data from over 14,000 students.

One reason that this is happening is because students are becoming more self-oriented as their world becomes increasingly more competitive. Some say that social networking is creating a more narcissistic generation. According to lead researchers, it is harder for today's college student to empathize with others because so much of their social interactions are done through a computer or cell phone and not through real life interaction. With their friends online they can pick and choose who they will respond to and who they will tune out. That is more than likely to carry over into real life.

This is also a generation that grew up playing video games. Much of their formative years development has been influenced by input from computer generated images and violent cyber-interactions. There has to be a connection. This may partly explain the numbing of this generation. Another point of view was presented by Christopher Lasch, a renowned and popular American historian, moralist, and social critic, in a book he published in 1979 called, The Culture of Narcissism: American Life in an Age of Diminishing Expectations. Lasch links the prevalence of narcissism in our society to the decline of the family unit, loss of core values, and long-term social disintegration in the twentieth century.

He believed that the liberal, utopian lifestyle of the 60's gave way to a search for personal growth in the 70's. But people were unsuccessful in their attempts to find their selves. So a movement began to build a society that celebrated self-expression, self-esteem, and self-love. That's all well and good, or so it seems, but as a result of the "me" focus, more narcissism was inadvertently created. It all backfired-aggression, materialism, lack of caring for others, and shallow values have been the result.

There are certainly many of us who have not become this way-studies speak for society in general. Today we live with constant internal and external pressures of life. On a daily basis our society faces terrorism, crime, economic crises, widespread job insecurity, war, political corruption. We see the disintegration of morality wherever we look.

As a writer, author, and inspirer I was greatly

disturbed by the overwhelming success of a book (I will not promote the name except to say that it has the word "gray" in the title) based on pornography and smut. It astounds me that millions of people have read it. If I were the publisher I would have instantly rejected a manuscript of such low moral content and offensive subject matter. Where has our appreciation for quality literature as a society gone to? And what has happened to our legal system? It has been demonstrated time and time again that the rights of the innocent take a back seat to the rights of the offender. Our laws do very little to control criminals. In fact, it seems as if criminals control the law. If ever an empathy disorder could spur unthinkable violence to erupt in a seemingly normal person, now is the time.

Emotional intelligence is learned through experience, reflection and modeling over a long period of time. Time must be set aside with someone you trust and respect that will allow you to experiment with and practice new behaviors, thoughts and feelings to the point of mastery. The environment needs to be supportive, emotionally engaging and offer time for practice.

If you are really interested in increasing your Self-Awareness, the following steps are necessary:

1. Acknowledge the fact that self-improvement is very vital.

2. Know the kind of person you want to be.

3. Realize your strengths, weakness and limitations as well as your values. Know what you stand for.

4. Find out about what people think of you, get feedback from people - who do people say you are , how you are perceived by others can be used to determine the gap between who you want to be and who you are presently.

5. Work with a supportive groups, encouraging people you trust (a coach is ideal) who can guide, teaches you and hold you accountable as you experiment with new thoughts, feelings and behavior in order to build on your strengths.

6. Put them into pracice , try out the new behaviors over time until your ideal self is realized. Increasing the three areas of Self-Awareness is worth the effort. It establishes the foundation upon which to build relationships and handle the challenges in your personal and professional life.

EMOTION AND INTELLIGENCE

Emotions and intelligence are indispensable terms and would be discussed throughout the length of this book. An understanding of these terms is important for an ensuing comprehension of EI (Alston, 2009). The Oxford English Dictionary defined emotion as "any agitation or disturbance of mind, feeling, passion; any vehement or excited mental state". Emotion is a neutral way to look at feelings, on the surface we can call emotions feeling. Among the circle of psychologists the definitions of emotions hardly varies as they all seem to agree. So, although you may feel "repelling" or weird, this is the part where a psychologist tries to detect if an emotion represents sadness, nervousness, irritability, anxiety or anger.

It is very easy to remember the difference between emotions and feelings with this idea: Emotions are the objective state of feelings. Emotions are clear, well-defined, and experienced by all people. Over the year Psychologists have identified several types of emotions that that has been expressed by humans. What they discovered is that you can also have a variety of emotions. A very good example to understanding what I mean by various types of emotions is when you think of mixing various ingredients or condiments together in the kitchen, when you combine flour, milk, vinegar and eggs, and then heat the mixture to make a pie. Now this is how two expressions of emotions can combine together, sometimes it might get a little complicated .Like how annoyance and irritation can combine to create rage if you don't check those emotions. Joy and excitement can lead to optimism. Feelings are the more prejudiced aspects of emotions, feelings can be hard to interprete. Some people are better at identifying their feelings than others are. You may find feelings less clear than emotions. For example, Julia overhears a co-worker telling someone that

Ted just got the job promotion Julia had applied for. She had been so sure that she was next in line for the job. As soon as she hears the news, Julia has a queasy, upset feeling in her stomach. She says she feels bloated, probably from something she ate. Although she believes she's feeling queasy — at least, that's her subjective experience — an outside observer could probably figure out that she really feels a bit traumatized and depressed. Now thats a narraive , another angle to look at it is that sometimes emotions overpower us because we draw them out of proportion we, make it seem bigger than usual. And this is what pessimistic thinkers do. They extend the negative emotion into broad areas of their lives. This is the quintessential "bring the office home" individual. I knew one executive who allowed anger at work to pervade all areas of his life.

Life happens. Events take place that are beyond our control, and some of them can be extremely upsetting and all-consuming. We can't avoid negative situations, nor can we change the behavior or opinions of other people involved. We can only look honestly at our own reactions and try to channel our responses into a positive direction.

Emotional balance is achieved through identifying, feeling and processing our emotional reactions in appropriate and healthy ways.

Here are some strategies to re-shape your reactions and find relief.

1. Briefly summarize the situation. Try to state what's happened as simply and unemotionally as possible, using concise and neutral language. Reducing your problem to its simplest form is a great way of making it seem smaller and more manageable.

For example, your mind may be screaming: "I can't believe she betrayed my trust! Why would she blab something I told her in strict confidence? She promised she wouldn't tell anyone. Now everyone is going to know! I'll never trust her again.

A simpler, calmer description would be: "I shared a secret with a friend who told it to someone else."

Restating the problem succinctly and neutrally takes away a lot of its drama and power. It also makes the situation seem less personal and unique. Lots of people fail to keep secrets and the world keeps turning. You can survive this.

2. Describe your current reaction to your challenge. How do you truly feel at this moment? Don't hold back. Are you angry, fearful, regretful, anxious, overwhelmed, defeated, resentful, or agitated? Get in touch with your true feelings. Acknowledge them; they belong to you and they are real.

3. Create a rating system (numbers, stars, plus signs, exclamation marks, etc.) and evaluate the intensity of your reaction. This is a form of validation and a way to judge where you are along the path of emotional healing.

4. Envision your desired emotional reaction. What's your concept of a healthy and appropriate response? How do you want to handle this situation? What kind of genuine reaction would make you feel like you handled yourself with dignity, fairness and grace?

5. Think about actions you can take to move closer to your desired reaction. For example, you may think

you owe someone an apology, even though you might not be ready to make it at this time.

Look at what role you played in creating the current situation. Do you need to change your attitude or perspective? Make the situation less personal or important? Or do you need to simply do nothing until a desirable course of action becomes clearer?

You may need to repeat these steps a number of times before you experience a calmer, more serene response. Keeping a journal may help you gain insight and see progress. Hopefully, with repetition and persistence you will streamline your path towards peace and emotional balance.

CRUSHING STRESS WITH EMOTIONAL INTELLIGENCE

Work stress is as old as work itself and so are the ways we respond. You can just imagine the first cave-clan's leader spending sleepless nights counting stalactites, worried about how he was going to break the news to UG and the other hunters that the decreasing wild beast population meant they were going to have less to eat.

Stress always has, and probably always will, go hand-in-hand with work.

Unfortunately, stress appears to be on the rise. In a study conducted earlier this year at the University of Rochester Medical Center in New York, Dr. Diana Fernandez, MD, found that job stress not only makes workers unhappier but also harms their health. In her study of 2,782 employees at a large manufacturing facility, Fernandez and her team found strong links between job stress and cardiovascular disease, depression, exhaustion, and weight gain. After a tense day of pink slips circulating around the office, many workers told Fernandez's team that they looked forward to going home and "vegging out" in front of the TV. In the American Psychological Association's 2009 Stress in America Survey, 42% of Americans said their stress levels had increased since the previous year. A lukewarm economy and high unemployment suggest that 2011's numbers aren't going to improve.

But what if you could reduce stress without having to wait for the economy to improve? A promising stream of research linking emotional intelligence (EQ) to stress-reduction offers exciting new clues about how to beat stress in spite of economic woes.

A team of Belgian researchers led by Dr. Moira Mikolajczak found that levels of emotional intelligence-a person's ability to understand and manage his or her own emotions and those of other people-determine how effectively people cope with stress. Mikolajczak found that people with high emotional intelligence report better moods, less anxiety, and less worry during times of tension and stress than those with less ability to identify and manage their emotions.

But emotional intelligence is not just about naïve optimism or disguising negative emotions by forcing yourself to put on a happy face. Emotionally intelligent people actually feel less stress. Emotionally intelligent people have improved their ability to engage their emotions and rational thinking simultaneously. This results in a more contained, comfortable reaction to stressful circumstances. As your EQ increases, you actually feel less stress.

Without consciously trying to control their reactions to stress, high EQ individuals show fewer physical signs of stress reactions, such as sweaty palms, elevated heart rate, and increased secretion of certain hormones and brain chemicals. When facing a situation that sends most people climbing up the walls, a high-EQ person approaches the stressor with the same calm composure that most people demonstrate only in the most trivial of circumstances.

In other words, emotionally intelligent people not only claim to experience less stress, they also physically and mentally experience less stress.

Why Emotional Intelligence Matters:

The Belgian researcher's uncovered two primary reasons for emotional intelligence limiting stress. First, they found that emotionally intelligent people evaluate their environment differently. In the words of Dr. Mikolajczak, they "are particularly inclined to look for the silver lining, invoke pleasant thoughts or memories in order to counter their current emotional state, think about what steps to take in order to handle the problem, and put it into perspective. In contrast, they seem less likely to catastrophize or to blame themselves for the occurrence of the problem and/or for their incapacity to solve it."

Second, and perhaps most important, people who are good with emotions are more likely to choose a "problem-focused" coping strategy. Each problem we encounter presents us with two choices: address the problem head-on or bury our heads in the sand, hoping that the issue will resolve itself. People who employ a problem-focused coping strategy devote their attention to solving the problem, rather than ignoring it. This adaptive approach to solving problems works to squash the cause of the stress and lessens the amount of stress experienced because the mere act of devising a plan makes you feel more relaxed and in control. People enjoy challenging jobs, crossword puzzles, and Sudoku for the same reason-solving problems is mentally stimulating.

In contrast, less emotionally intelligent people let their fear and anxiety drive them toward a "problem-avoidance" coping strategy, which only prolongs the tension. As you might guess, these two strategies become a self-fulfilling prophecy-confirming the belief that led the individual to think that way in the first place and furthering his or her conviction that the problem is too much to handle. The habit of avoiding problems doesn't make you forget them. Instead, it keeps you wallowing in the negative emotions that accompany a burdensome challenge. The problem itself remains a perpetual source of stress, amplifying the bad feelings that make stress hard to deal with.

In theory, it would seem that you could take a shortcut by skipping the emotional intelligence piece and just learning the adaptive coping strategies. The only problem is that people who aren't good with emotions are also poor at using a problem-focused strategy. Only the emotionally intelligent bunch-who know how to fend off the distractions created by fear, sadness, anger, jealousy, shame, and the like-are able to effectively implement a problem-focused approach.

EQ Training: The Gift That Keeps On Giving:

Fortunately, virtually anyone can develop emotional intelligence with training. The Belgian team proved that emotional intelligence could be significantly improved with only a handful of short training sessions. In a series of four 150-minute trainings spread out over a month, participants significantly increased their ability to identify and manage emotions. The trainings included such basic training elements as short lectures, role-playing, group discussions, reading assignments, and a daily journal entry about one emotional experience.

Most amazing, however, is that the people who received emotional intelligence training not only maintained their new emotional intelligence skills six months after the training ended but also showed a slight improvement in their EQ at the six-month follow-up. We can only imagine how much they would have improved had they received even a brief reminder to practice their emotional intelligence skills every few days.

How To Beat Your Stress:

To start reducing your stress by improving your own emotional intelligence, there are two basic steps.

1. Get an EQ education. The best way to educate yourself is with the help of a reputable, certified emotional intelligence trainer or coach. If you check with your training department, you might already have access to such a professional within your organization.

2. Practice. After you have developed the right foundation of emotional intelligence knowledge, you must practice using it. You can do this with the old-fashioned system of sticky notes on your nightstand and bathroom mirror, or you can get a little more precise with an automated reminder system.

In sum, the research you've just explored means that people-all people-are very capable of eradicating stress with a relatively small amount of emotional intelligence training. A little emotional intelligence training goes a very long way in helping you to reduce stress and handle the obstacles that life inevitable throws your way.

ROLE OF EMPATHY IN LIFE

Empathy plays great role in our life in almost every sphere. The skill of empathy, though we inherit it, can be cultivated, which plays a significant role in making us successful in those spheres. Role of empathy in the life of an individual is actually dependent on its conceptualization by the individual, which varies widely. Nevertheless, empathy acts to reflect what has been perceived and creates a supportive or confirming atmosphere. Empathy is a powerful communication skill that is actually underused by many. It allows one to understand thoughts and resultant feelings created by them in others. Empathy also makes one to respond to other's feelings sympathetically so that they can win their trust, which promotes communication further. Our fear of failure, anger, and frustration suddenly drop away, allowing for a more meaningful dialogue and a deepening of relationships.

Empathy is more than simple sympathy, which makes the individual understand others with compassion and sensitivity. That is why it is plays an important role in the workplace, where many people work together to achieve something of significance. It helps create deep respect for the co-workers, thereby fostering a harmonious atmosphere in the workplace. Similarly, empathy is helpful in our professional life because, besides facilitating communication, it makes us a sympathetic listener to our clients, whereby we are able to understand them better. Because empathy makes us able to communicate effectively and listen empathetically, we stand a better chance of making our personal and social relationships successful. In fact, empathy is capable of nurturing every kind of relationship we enter into or are in. As it is clear that empathy affects our life with far reaching ramifications, we should help our children to develop this inborn trait so that they can become better human beings for themselves and for the world. Since empathy promotes pro-social behavior, it will help our children develop close relationships, maintain friendships and develop better communities. Emotional intelligence has assumed great importance over the past twenty years as an instrument in developing an ability to work with our own and other's emotions. One of the most important components of emotional intelligence skills is empathy.

Undoubtedly, empathy immensely affects our everyday life. This trait will come in handy in situations, where we find ourselves trapped, because it will make us understand other's perspectives. While it's true that we are born with this trait and it's in unnaturally, it happens to be underused by many. As empathy is one of the most important skills to be practiced for success in everyday life, we should encourage our children to cultivate it.

Empathy is an inherent trait in humans but it is present in changeable extent in us. That is why everyone doesn't empathize to others to the same extent and in the same way. Nevertheless, it plays a significant role in our day-to-day life, contributing extensively to our personal, professional and social success.

EMOTIONAL MATURITY AND EMOTIONAL INTELLIGENCE

Emotional maturity moves beyond "intelligence" to a higher state of consciousness, guided by what one senses, feels and intuits, and one's heart.

Five principles underlie emotional maturity:

1 - Every negative emotion we experience right here and right now is actually a childhood reaction applied to a current person, circumstance or event.

2 - Most adult's are 3-4-5-year-olds in adult bodies wearing adult clothes.

3 - No one can make you feel a way you don't want to feel. You hold the power to how you want to feel.

4 - An adult can be emotionally mature and child-like or immature and child-ish.

5 - Mindfulness, focus and presence are the keys to emotional maturity.

First, emotional maturity begins with an exploration of how emotional make-up forms early on in life, based on interactions with our primary caregivers, then with extended family, teachers, friends, clergy, etc. Around seven, our psychological and emotional "programming" is set. Our reactivity (e.g., anger, sadness, fear, shame, hurt, guilt and loneliness, etc.) to people, events and circumstances that triggered us early in life is stored in our cells, and arises when "related" triggers appear later in life.

The emotionally mature adult identifies and experiences emotions without acting out, or stuffing or suppressing them. Some emotionally intelligent, but "immature," adults," knowing about emotions, are often unable to appropriately identify or manage emotions. Rather, they resort to "defended" reactivity, sidestepping their emotions: intellectualizing, explaining, analyzing, disagreeing, attacking, flattering, joking, apologizing, evading, going silent, becoming aloof or suspicious, rejecting, criticizing, judging, etc. These emotionally intelligent, but immature, folks come across as: superior, arrogant, stubborn, defiant, hostile, people-pleasing, wishy-washy, phony, resentful, intolerant, self-pitying or victimized, etc. Not mature behavior. When we explore the nature of our emotions, we move towards a "that was then; this is now" perspective, becoming less triggered by current events and circumstances. We don't "futurize" our past.

Secondly, not exploring the developmental nature of emotions, many aren't aware that childhood emotions play out in "adult" life - that we bring our "family" to our adult interactions - at work, at home, at play and in relationship. Our adult reactivity to people, places, circumstances and events that push our buttons is actually an "unconscious" reminder of childhood people, places, circumstances and events. For the emotionally immature individual their paradigm is "that was then; this is still then." Their past leaks out on to current situations.

Third. When we "work" to understand the nature of our emotions, we "get" that, as a child, we reacted the way we reacted to either feel safe and secure, or to receive acknowledgment, approval and love. The emotionally mature adult is not a child in an adult body, wearing adult clothes and does not react as a child. The emotionally mature adult understands "my emotions are not me, but mine; I'm in control, not my emotions." In this place of non-judgment, we experience an event with greater objectively, optimally with no emotional charge or at least with less emotional charge. Emotional maturity teaches us how to detach from a person, place, and event or circumstance that would normally trigger reactivity. Here, we can remain in a state of equanimity or manageable or aware arousal. In this place, we don't choose to blame a person or thing for "making me feel" a certain way.

Fourth. Our behavior is always vacillating between the ends of two continua: (1) the child-like, emotionally mature adult and (2) the child-ish, emotionally immature adult. What do these look like? The "child-like" qualities of an emotionally-mature adult include: lively, excited, alive, juicy, adventurous, joyful, happy, open etc. The "adult" qualities of an emotionally-mature adult include: nurturing/supportive, firm/fair, helpful, respectful, self-responsible, non-judgmental, heart-felt, honest, sincere, allowing, accepting, focused on well-be-ing; one serves, coaches or mentors. On the other hand, the "child-ish" qualities of an emotionally immature adult include: reactive, acting out, throwing tantrums, fearful, scared, needy, angry, resentful, pushy, bullying, jealous, envious, shut down, quiet, withdrawn, defensive, argumentative and grandiose, etc. The "adult" qualities of an emotionally immature adult include: non-loving, overbearing, micromanaging, controlling, disrespectful, fearful, angry, negative, judgmental, critical, abusive (mentally, emotionally, psychologically, physically), dishonest, insincere, narcissistic and focused on the self and the ego. The question, "How old do I feel right now?" can support one to experience where they are on the continua in any given moment.

Fifth, The most visible and effective outcome of emotional maturity is our ability to be in the moment, in our body and present (non-reactive, non-judgmental). We track our emotions in our body. We don't "do" anything, "fix" anything, or change anything as we witness and observe our emotions rise and fall. Being present to our emotions allows our True Self (not our mind) to drive as our Heart and Soul inform us of "right knowing," "right understanding" and "right action." We have the emotion without "becoming" the emotion. We understand the "trigger" for my reactivity may be "outside" me, but the "cause" of my emotions is within. So, we watch, witness and observe as we're triggered and allow our True Self to support our inner journey and exploration, with curiosity, not efforting or mentally changing our experience. Mindfulness, presence, focus, trust and surrender to our emotional experience bring about whatever is needed in the moment. Our Heart and Soul never call for negativity or reactivity, but a considered, emotionally mature response.

In our never-ending journey of unfolding our infinite potential, emotional maturity can be thought of as a next step in the evolution of our humanity and the opening of greater, conscious awareness to our self and to others.

FUNDAMENTALS OF EMOTIONAL INTELLIGENCE

Those fundamentals include: self-awareness, self-regulation, motivation, empathy and social skills. We can spend our lives accumulating degrees, job experiences and the many certifications that we seem to need more of, but in reality, long lasting success comes from within us. Some call it wisdom. You might argue that wisdom is something that cannot be developed, it must come to us. In some cases that may be true. However, EQ or emotional intelligence can be developed and worked upon. This in turn will help us use our best thinking, and come up with the more reasonable decisions, and this in turn will help us be wiser.

Most of us have various strengths and opportunities when it comes to the building blocks of emotional intelligence. If possible, It is advisable that you take an some tests and find out how you fair compared to others. You may be surprised by the results and discover that you have strengths in areas you might not have suspected. And you may also discover that you have weak points and attributes that are holding you back from professional and personal success. However, even if you don't have the opportunity to take an assessment to learn your particularly strengths and opportunities, it can be helpful to get an understanding of the ingredients of emotional intelligence and get some ideas on how they might be strengthened.

Self-awareness as we defined earlier is the ability to recognize and understand your moods, emotions, and drives as well as understanding their effect on others. You're able to understand your limitations, strengths and emotions and then self-manage. With self-awareness, you can reduce negative leadership traits and express yourself better. You're also more likely to have higher stress tolerance and restraint. You're less likely to lose control and cause workers distress when you're frustrated or dealing with stress and/or change. This means you know how you are feeling and why. It also involves having a sense of your self-worth and your strengths. Suggestions for improving your self-awareness include. Pay serious attention to your behaviors and see if you recognize patterns throughout the day, reflect on the connection between your emotions and your behavior. Write in a journal about your emotional responses to situations that were significant. Share your introspective discoveries with a family member or trusted friend. Make a list of your strengths and areas for improvement. Look at it on a daily basis.

Self-regulation is defined as the ability to control or redirect disruptive impulses and moods and the propensity to suspend judgment and think before acting. This involves keeping your disruptive emotions and impulses in check. It involves taking personal accountability for your actions. And, it is the ability to be comfortable with new ideas, approaches, and ways of doing things. Suggestions to improving your ability to self-regulate include:

Practice self-restraint by listening first, pausing and then responding. When becoming frustrated, identify what brought on that emotion. Create effective responses to stressful situations by finding strategies for altering a negative mood. Discuss ways of dealing with change and stress with family members, friends or a trusted advisor. Focus on events that provide a sense of calm or positive emotions. Motivation as it relates to EQ is defined as a passion to work for reasons that go beyond money or status and a propensity to pursue goals with energy and persistence. This involves a readiness to act on opportunities. It also means that you are persistent in pursuing your goals despite encountering many obstacles. Ways to improve your EQ motivation include the following practices:

Set specific goals with dates for achievement. Clarify why these goals are important to you. Ask yourself not only, "What are my goals?" but also, "Why are they my goals?"

Work with a peer or trusted advisor to create detailed action items to work toward your overall goals. Set aside time to work on your goals each day, even if it is just five minutes at a time. List your goals and post them where you can see them every day.

Empathy is defined as the ability to understand the emotional make up of other people. This is your ability to sense others' feelings and perspectives and taking an active interest in their concerns. It is also the ability to cultivate opportunities through different kinds of people. It helps you anticipate, recognize and meet the needs of others. You can learn to practice more empathy by doing some of the following:

Attempt to understand others before communicating your point of view.

Observe nonverbal behavior to evaluate the negative or positive emotions of others.

Watch interactions of other people that you determine to be empathetic. What can you do to model that behavior?

Break bad interpersonal habits, such as interrupting others. Observe body language for nonverbal messages being expressed. Seek clarification from others when attempting to read emotional responses. Be nonjudgmental in your interactions with others. Social skills are a proficiency in managing relationships and building networks. These skills help you work with others toward shared goals and create group synergy in pursuing collective goals. They help you listen openly and send convincing messages, while negotiating and dissolving disagreements. You can improve your social skills by:

 ✓ Being aware of the message your body language is communicating.

 ✓ Asking those you admire to describe their experience when socializing with you.

Remembering people's names. Everyone has a hard time with it. Use memory techniques and be known as the one that remembers! After making a mistake, take accountability quickly and find ways to make amends. Taking notice when emotions are taking over an interaction and then find ways to remove yourself from the situation. Showing a genuine curiosity for others' well-being

EMPATHY VS EMOTIONAL INTELLIGENCE

Empathy is the ability to feel what the other person is feeling. It is to experience their emotions. It is the ability to put yourself in the other person's shoes in a big and meaningful way. Emotional intelligence is the ability to manage your own emotions, as well as the emotions of others. This is a skill that all great communicators possess (more about this tomorrow).Empathy and emotional intelligence work together in sales, enabled by caring, to produce long-lasting relationships. Together they are the foundation of trust.

Empathy in general would mean feeling what the other person is feeling and 'being in the shoes of the other'. Empathy creates emotional link and involvement and could be between lovers, family members, friends, or even strangers. Empathy relates to contentedness and a sense of just knowing what another person is feeling. Some individuals are simply more empathetic than others whereas some individuals could find it hard to relate. Some questions that psychology would deal with are what creates empathy and why are some individuals more empathetic than others.

Empathy or a feeling of contentedness and being in the shoes of others is closely related to intuition as intuition helps in the understanding and recognition of emotions in others. Even if emotions are covert and not manifested, empathy helps in identifying these emotions through intuition. Empathy is thus described as recognizing other people's emotions through intuition and is marked by a feeling of connecting to the other person.

In any leadership situation such as in political leadership and social leadership, it is necessary for leaders to feel certain degree of empathy with the other members of the group as the leaders have to feel connected to the followers to make an impact in their opinions and decisions. Teachers also have to feel empathy with the students as this creates a contentedness without which the teaching experience is meaningless both for the teachers and the students. Empathy is about motivating or influencing the other person by tapping in on his or her emotions. It is easier to influence or change people if you are keenly aware of what they are thinking or feeling as this helps to predict the possible responses. Finally we have understanding of other people only when we are able to predict their responses and empathy adds a predictive quality to the interaction.

Stages Of Empathy

We can say that empathy starts with intuition and ends with prediction, and prediction is when one person is able to foretell the emotional responses of the other. The stages of empathy are thus given as:

1. Intuition

2. Connection

3. Consideration

4. Prediction

5. Motivation

The first stage of intuition involves one person naturally intuitive towards the other as with intuition of the other person's emotions and feelings or thought processes; the next stage of empathy or a feeling of connection is created. The connection between two people naturally leads to a feeling of mutual consideration and the next stage of predicting each other's responses to situation. In some cases empathy could be mutual although in many cases as in a relationship between a therapist and her patient, the empathy could be one sided. After the connection is established and there is a deep sense of consideration for the others feelings, and an understanding as to why the person is feeling in a particular way, one person who empathizes with the other is able to move to the next stage of predicting the emotional responses. Understanding the response patterns in other people is an essential part of connecting and relating to them closely and would definitely suggest the ability of being in the shoes of the other. The last stage of empathy deals with the more directional aspect as in the case of teacher or therapist there is a need to motivate or influence the other person following an empathetic connection. In fact the empathy may have been established to influence the other person to attain some goals or reach some targets. So influencing and motivating the other person is an integral part of empathy and is a tacit goal of empathetic relations.

Apart from the five stages of empathy discussed, empathy could involve subsequent feelings of friendship, love, rapport, admiration, dependence and this would depend on whether the empathy is between a teacher and a student, a therapist and a patient, a leader and his followers or between lovers or friends. From a psychological point of view, empathy would involve fulfilling the safety and security needs of other individuals and also their love and a sense of belonging. Our need for Empathy are thus somewhere in between the love-attachment-belongingness (psychological) needs of individuals and the safety-security needs of individuals and the need for empathy exists in every individual and is manifested in both the forms of giving and receiving empathy.

Individuals fulfill their love and find a sense of belonging, needs created by relating to others and empathy uses love and belongingness to provide safety and security. Thus the purpose of empathy as explained with Maslow's hierarchy of needs theory is to make the other person happy by providing a sense of security and lending support as is the goal of empathy could mean a positive influence of one person on the other. Empathy highly enhances social interaction as it adds elements of familiarity, connectedness and consideration between people and help to instill and maintain human values.

WHY IS EMOTIONAL INTELLIGENCE IMPORTANT?

An emotionally intelligent individual is both highly conscious of his or her own emotional states, even negativity—frustration, sadness, or something more subtle—and able to identify and manage them. These people are also especially tuned in to the emotions others experience. It's easy to see how a sensitivity to emotional signals from within and from the social environment could make one a better friend, parent, leader, or romantic partner. Fortunately, these skills can be honed.

Many people are not completely aware how important emotional intelligence is in their lives. We attempt to read many books and articles about this matter just for the knowledge, but we ignore the fact that if we apply emotional intelligence in our daily life and work, it could lead us to somewhere else that we never expected.

The key skills of emotional intelligence could be learned by anyone, at any time. Imagine if you are able to overcome, control and get over your daily life stress with just being emotionally aware of everything that goes right there around you.

Emotional intelligence could be summarized in the ability to express your emotions and to control them at the same time, understand and interpret to others feelings.

There are four easy steps that can lead you to the emotional intelligence you always wished to have;

The first one is sensing the emotions: you should concentrate and accurately perceive the message someone tries to tell you, this actually involves not only understanding the person's intended words but also watching the non-verbal signs, body language and facial expressions.

The second one is reasoning with emotions: we should use our emotions to promote thinking. Emotions help in prioritizing what we pay attention and react to. This means that emotions play a very big part in guiding our minds to believing things that might or might not happen. We naturally react to things that attract our minds.

The third one is understanding emotions: emotions may carry whole different meanings at many times, some people can express their anger in an indirect way, this can actually be very obvious in the example of the angry boss; he can scream, shout and give you a very hard time just because he has an issue related to your work, or he experienced a bad morning with his wife. We should never get confused in understanding the reasons behind people's reactions and that's why training yourself to have emotional intelligence can help you in this matter.

The fourth and last one is managing emotions (the ability to manage your emotions): Emotions are valuable, and offer a bounty of benefits. Once we're able to process and cope with them effectively, we can then learn a lot about ourselves and our needs. If you feel something, let it out, do not engage yourself in another action hoping you can distract your feelings, this can lead you to many problems.

Managing and controlling your emotions and feelings are very important; it is a step towards reaching the emotional intelligence of knowing how to perfectly understand people around you with the least words and actions they make.

Despite the fact that emotional intelligence lacks the volume of quantitative empirical cognitive research that IQ has, the research in the field of cognitive learning has suggested that emotional intelligence is a key fundamental aspect of learning. According to a report published by the National Center for Clinical Infant Programs, the level of success that a student has learning new material boils down to their individual levels of confidence, self-control, curiosity, their ability to communicate, their cooperativeness, their elatedness and their intentionality. All these traits are aspects of emotional intelligence.

More recently social scientists are beginning to uncover the relationship of emotional intelligence to other organizational psychologies, such as leadership, group performance, individual performance, interpersonal exchange, performance evaluations, and change management. Humans are social beings and as such our level of success when dealing with people is intimately linked with our level of emotional intelligence.

Our Heart and Soul never call for negativity or reactivity, but a considered, emotionally mature response.

In our never-ending journey of unfolding our infinite potential, emotional maturity can be thought of as a next step in the evolution of our humanity and the opening of greater, conscious awareness to our self and to others.

So, some questions for self-reflection are:

Do you ever feel you need to change the way you respond to others?

How do you feel when others challenge or disagree with you?

Do you find yourself feeling fearful, angry or anxious? Do you know why?

How do you respond to others' feedback?

Are you ever taken back by the way you react to others?

Do you ever feel afraid about exploring your emotions? Why?

Do you consider yourself to be emotionally mature? What would others say?

IMPROVING YOUR LEVEL OF EMOTIONAL INTELLIGENCE

Researches and scientists see the intelligence quotient, also known as I.Q., as fixed, meaning that it does not change throughout one's lifetime. E.I. differs greatly from I.Q. in that E.I. can be improved through a combination of life experience, maturity, conscious thought and perseverance. You can improve your level of emotional intelligence by doing the following:

Reflect back to the most recent time you can remember of when you had hurt somebody's feelings when they got close to you and trusted you, study what your reactions were at the time and analyze what you said that inflicted emotional pain on the other person. Try to put yourself in shoes of the other person' and empathize with them, try to feel what they feel like you were in that position. In this drill, you will effectively increase your understanding of empathy thereby increasing your level of emotional intelligence as a result. Rather than you finding fault with others, work on developing a mindset of positive thoughts and try to come up with possible solutions on a given problem. Remember that everyone you deal with is human and as humans we make mistakes.

Also by being human we have the ability to learn from

our mistakes and by creating a positive attitude we can effectively coach other people and ourselves to move forward instead of blaming other people or events for mistakes. Then you should now come to the realization that in order to succeed in this game we call life, it becomes important to have a high level of one to one communication with those the people around you. You are, for the most part, helpless without other people to help you along the way. By better understanding their emotional needs you will be able to communicate with them more effectively and more accurately thus paving the way to your own personal success.

What You Need To Be Emotionally Mature

1. The ability to deal constructively with reality

To deal with reality in a constructive manner, we must face truth, the facts, rather than deny them. Running from problems or hoping they do not exist does not make them go away. Regardless of how unpleasant they may be at times, facing the facts is the first step to dealing with any situation. When people have difficulty facing reality, they resort to all sorts of unhealthy ways to deal with the unpleasant feelings and pain. They try to soothe themselves with alcohol, drugs, or any other way that temporarily masks their reality and pain. There are healthy and constructive ways to cope that lead to greater emotional maturity and growth. It may not be the easiest path to take, but it leads to healing, lasting comfort and hope.

2. The capacity to adapt to change

Change is not always easy. It can turn our world upside down at times and cause a great deal of stress. Whether the change is minor, like having to change our plans for the day, or more significant, such as moving to a new home, changing jobs, getting married or divorced, adapting to change is to make necessary adjustments. Sometimes the most important adjustment is in our attitude. Change can annoy us as it disrupts our routine and expectations, but we can choose to accept it and allow ourselves time to get comfortable with change.

3. A relative freedom from symptoms that are produced by tensions and anxieties

The symptoms produced from tensions and anxieties can include physical distress (headaches, stomach problems, rapid heart rate) and emotional distress (worry, restlessness, panic). Anxiety is a major mental health problem affecting millions of people every day. It negatively affects all levels of people's lives--their mental and physical health, relationships, work. To live free of its destructive symptoms and consequences is to cope with life stress in a healthy manner, learn to relax, release worries, and develop inner peace.

4. The capacity to find more satisfaction in giving than receiving

People who give of themselves--their time, attention, help, finances, or what they are able-- are generally more fulfilled and happy than those who do not. People who are primarily takers are more likely to use others for their own personal gain and are often considered selfish, stingy, and/or greedy. Like the old scrooge, they end up miserable. Givers, on the other hand, want to contribute and make a positive difference in this world. It is healthy to give cheerfully and willingly as it contributes to our sense of purpose and helps us connect with others and our society.

5. The capacity to relate to other people in a consistent manner with mutual satisfaction and helpfulness

Like I always say, life is all about relationships. We relate to others every single day--whether it is a relative, co-worker, neighbor, or stranger, our lives are intertwined with others. Love and respect are two key factors to relating successfully to others. Unlike dysfunctional relationships, healthy relationships are stable and provide deep satisfaction and joy.

6. The capacity to sublimate, to direct one's instinctive hostile energy into creative and constructive outlets

If we were to release all our frustrations and anger on the world, we would have a hostile existence. Instead, we can take that energy and direct it into something good and productive. It has long been said that sports is a great outlet of extra energy. Anything that is positive, constructive and creative can redirect our energies and put them to good use. A basketball player once told me that the court is where all his angry energy was released. He redirected his hostile energy in an acceptable way within specific guidelines and limits. It gave him a constructive outlet and helped him to really enjoy what he was doing without hurting others and/or himself.

7. The capacity to love, Love is the greatest power in the world

There's hardly any exact definition for love, because its that inexplicable beautiful feeling As humans, we are born with the capacity to love. The greatest differences between us are how we communicate our love.

Self-love is not opposed to the love of other people. You cannot really love yourself and do yourself a favor without doing people a favor, and vise versa. ~Karl Menninger

Experience is not what happens to you, it's how you interpret what happens to you. ~Aldous Huxley

Maturity has more to do with what types of experiences you've had, and what you've learned from them, and less to do with how many birthdays you've celebrated. ~unknown

TYPES OF EMOTIONAL INTELLIGENCE

Emotional Intelligence consists of five basic components namely self-awareness, self-regulation, motivation, empathy and social skills. The first three competencies are intra-personal and concern your ability to know and manage yourself. Empathy and social skills are inter-personal competencies and concern your ability to interact and get along with others. The better your intra-personal skills, the easier it becomes to express your inter-personal skills. Mastering these skills will allow you to live a better, happier and more successful and fulfilled life.

Self-awareness is the first component of emotional intelligence. It is the ability to know which emotions you are feeling and why. When you understand your emotions, it is easier for you to acknowledge and control your emotions and prevent your feelings from ruling you. You also become more confident as you do not let your emotions get out of control. Being self-aware also enables you to take an honest look at yourself and better know your strengths and weaknesses, and work on these areas to achieve better outcomes for yourself and others.

Recognizing our own emotions and how they recognize our own thoughts and behavior is what is essential for proper performance in workplace. Knowing our strengths and weakness and developing self-confidence is the prime for success in career.

Self-Regulation is the ability to control your emotions and impulses and choose the emotions that you want to experience instead of being the victim of whatever emotions arise. In self regulation you are a complete master over your emotions and when you are able to manage your emotional state, it becomes easier for you to think before you act and this prevents you from making impulsive and careless decisions. This skill also allows you to transform negative exhausting emotions into more positive and productive ones. Regulating ourselves is an essential component of Emotional intelligence. It is important to manage change that life brings in and for this we require self-regulation. Changes are the one which never change and so regulating ourselves to adapt to the new and different environ is essential.

Motivation :The third component of emotional intelligence is motivation. This is about using your emotions to remain positive, optimistic and persistent rather than negative and pessimistic. When you have a high degree of emotional intelligence you tend to be very motivated, productive and efficient in everything they do. You also use your emotions positively to take the right actions to persist and achieve your goals even in the face of considerable adversity or difficulty. Motivation is the ability to remain optimistic and to keep ourselves going even in case of failures and setbacks is called as motivation. Motivation is that internal power that you find when there is no reason to move foward, its that feeling you have after you have failed that makes you want to keep trying even when it looks stupid. Motivation is the one which makes us move towards our goals and desire. Facing organizational commitments, learning to improve performance, setting up challenging goals and being ready to seize opportunities is the most essential in today's corporate environment. All these can be done only through motivation.

The combination of all these competencies together make up the Emotional Intelligence quotient and possessing these skills are very important to succeed in the highly competitive, fast-moving, hi-tech world.

The corporate industries we have in the world today demands something more than powerful IQ. It sustains and takes hold of any individual with various social and personal competencies that allow them to regulate and manage the emotions of themselves and others around them. This ability to regulate the emotions with respect to the environment is known as Emotional Intelligence

Empathy is the fourth component of emotional intelligence. It is the ability to truly recognize and understand the feelings and point of view of people around you. Empathetic people usually possess the ability to listen effectively and accurately to others and are usually very excellent at managing relationships, improving communication; building trust and relating with others. Empathetic people are people you want to open up to , they have a way of making you talk about deep things you never want to talk about ,they are good listeners and if you are empathetic then it means You're able to understand the needs, wants and feelings of your subordinates and their situational issues. Having empathy, you're more likely to know what motivates workers to be more productive and pleased with their jobs, its like you've studied them and can feel what goes on in their head. You also have more of a team mindset and you , which means you're more open to improving team relationships and environmental issues that affect health and productivity. You can also better recognize desired traits in job candidates.

The fifth component of emotional intelligence are social skills. People with Social skills are the life of a party, emotionally intelligent people have good social skills and are excellent at building and maintaining relationships. When you are highly emotionally intelligent, you no longer focus on your own success first and you always have other's best interests in mind, you are constantly trying to see what you can do for people, what you can contribute. You always promote an environment where people cooperate with each other instead of compete with one another and you always help others develop and grow.

BENEFIT OF EMOTIONAL INTELLIGENCE

Your emotional intelligence (EI) is the ability to control and use your emotions in a constructive and productive manner.Its about making the best use of emotions to your benefit and to the benefit of others. It is very important to leadership and for successful relationships and I would advice anyone planning on taking leadership responsibilities to get trained properly in the use of emotional intelligence. It's your ability to intuitively communicate so effectively that you inspire others while not being derailed by upsetting or extreme circumstances to respond most appropriately as opposed to react in haste. Most times leaders are usually hated by their subordinate because they fail to consider the feelings, they use their powers and authority as superiors to behave irrational towards their staffs and this is because they are not emotionally intelligent, emotional intelligent leaders are loved by the staff because they have a way of correcting their subordinates without ridiculing them. Leaders who are strong in this skill have good emotional self-control, think clearly even when they are experiencing strong emotions, and make decisions using both their heart and their head. This does not mean they don't have sensual feelings. On the other hand they are passionate people just like you and I. However, they understand that a man in passion can sometimes get in the way of their personality, making them tough as a nail and hard to relate to so they need temper their passion immediately.

Along with the general competencies for various job roles, you may want to focus on your company's key competencies and this is where emotional intelligence skills come in again. If your company focuses on great customer service, for example, you may want to focus on customer service-related competencies. Likewise, if your company's progress is centered on fast innovation, this would suggest a greater emphasis on creativity and innovation competencies. Leaders high in emotional intelligence are connected to the people around them. They present as authentic and empathetic, willing to practice expansive thinking, constantly seeking to include and understand rather than exclude and ignore. This means resilient and empowering leadership that isn't afraid of others opinions and doesn't feel the urge to have the final decision or always be proved correct. These leaders are centred and in control of both themselves and the world around them, which inspires confidence and trust, creating an atmosphere where employees energetically collaborate to produce the best possible results for the business.

The question is - who do we think of when we reflect on our own personal experiences of emotionally intelligent leadership? The sad truth is that, for most of us at least, there's a relative paucity of these people in the places we work. The majority of businesses still thinks of emotions and feelings as valueless and reward people not for HOW they get results but WHAT results they deliver. As a result, when we consider our own experiences, we are far more likely to recall distracted and busy leaders that don't have time to listen or who don't really listen even when they're sitting in front of us watching our mouths move.

The good news is emotionally intelligent leaders are not a fictional narrative , they are out there in organizations somewhere; and some companies are even investing and looking to foster and encourage leaders in their organizations. These businesses not exactly doing anything beyond the ordinary but they're simply accepting that there is a better way of doing things. They believe that creating a better place to work is achievable, and that assessing and developing the necessary skills is very much easy and achievable, it's has actually been a tried and tested practice that has been around for years.

These organizations are constantly looking to determine and instil the five components that all emotionally intelligent leaders should have in common; we have discussed these components in previous chapters. They are trying to build leaders who:

1. Understand and read the meaning behind thier own feelings

2. Can effectively express what they feel

3. Can 'Tap into' their feelings and into the emotions of others, especially their subordinates and leaders

4. Manage facts and feelings to yield great results

5. Positively influence their own and the feelings of others

In order to hold effective emotional intelligence you must first be self-aware, we have talked about this component earlier. In a culture focused on quantifiable deliverable, that is making it big with the number of sales, decreased production time, increased cost benefits, etc. Self-reflection isn't a priority. I say make it a priority before it costs you money, your job or valuable relationships.

Why is it important to have emotional intelligence? The first and simplest reason I can give you is that it builds confidence. Self-assurance grows with heightened self-awareness to a life driven by purpose and an ability to execute one's goals for a greater good. Confidence is essential for healthy relationships and communication unhampered by disruptive, self-destructive emotions. So if your behavior in certain situations is predictably ineffective and unfulfilling, improve your emotional intelligence the same way you build other skills, by learning and practicing.

Most of us call it gut feeling, but now psychologists are calling those feelings emotional intelligence or EI. Emotional intelligence is something like your IQ. Your IQ score doesn't tell you how much you know it simply tells you what your capacity to learn and comprehend is. Your EI is a tad trickier to measure and there is a great deal of disagreement on how it should be done. However, scientists can agree that in general, people who have a high EI, meaning they can identify their own emotions and the emotions of others, tend to have certain behaviors. Here's a quick list of some of those behaviors.

1. Adaptability

Developing emotional intelligence allows an individual to understand the emotions or motives of others and as a result they are more willing to adapt to a situation than a person who can only understand what they personally are feeling.

2. Managing emotions in others

As we have mood swings, excessive ego, and emotional breakdown and stress it is best that we keep everything simple. So that we don't flare up and hurt other people, managing emotions is not really about us despite the facts that we have a lot on our plate, its about understanding that the emotions in others is a key leadership trait which allows the person with high EI to influence others. Understanding needs and feelings lends itself to developing courses of action that will fulfill those needs and at the same time accomplish what the leader wants accomplished.

3. Emotional control

Persons who have a high EI understand their own emotions and can analyze them rationally. So when they are faced with frustration or fear or anger, they are less likely to react to them instinctively and are more likely to act in a controlled and informed manner. Emotional control can sometimes be developed with emotional maturity , well there are quite a number of younger individuals who have been able to master emotional control than many adults. Emotional control keeps you in check and discipline you , it takes so much intentional effort to achieve this feat.

4. Less Impulsive

High Emotional Inteligence means bad news for marketers who take opportunity of people's impulse to buy products. People with high EI don't react impulsively but rather look at their feelings and make rational decisions without the interference of overwhelming emotional pull.

5. Strong relationships

Maybe one of the greatest advantages of elevated emotional intelligence is the ability to enter into and sustain strong and fulfilling relationships. Being able to understand and appreciate the emotions of others and not being driven by a "me first" need can result in more satisfying and less conflictive interactions with the people around you.

6. More optimistic face it.

We live in a culture that sees the glass half empty more than we see it half full. High EI develops high self-esteem which in turn gives the person the confidence to see the brighter side even in difficult situations.

7. Better stress management

Precisely because they have more self-esteem, self-confidence and an optimistic viewpoint of life, people with developed EI can handle more stress and pressure than others. Being able to identify stress points not as threats but simply as challenges to be met, changes the nature of the stress to a manageable condition. There are obvious advantages to developing emotional intelligence but there are also arguments over how that can be done. Some say it is simply an innate skill that you are born with. Others say you can improve it through training programs like emotional intelligence workshops. Whatever the answer is, it's obvious that understanding ourselves and the emotions of others has a distinct advantage in communications, relationships and personal behavior.

EMOTIONAL INTELLIGENCE FOR LEADERS

It is usually easier to identify those who have high EQ. These people are very self-aware and take the time to reflect on their actions and emotions. They recognize what triggers certain emotions and how to handle them even under dire circumstances. They also know when they may have reached a "boiling point" and need to back off from a situation temporarily, review what has happened, and devise a solution. It is like hitting the pause button on a remote control.

In addition, they understand that for one to develop emotionally there are times when they may face criticism from others and they need to see this as an opportunity for growth; in other words it is viewed as a learning lesson. They are also willing to provide feedback to others on their team, but they do it in a manner that is helpful not hurtful. These individuals are also sensitive to others' feelings, so they know when they may have overstepped and need to offer an apology. This does take courage because many would rather avoid a situation versus getting into a conflict with another team member. It is much trickier to figure out those who have low EQ. Some may have excellent technical skills and have been successful in their career so far but when a crisis occurs they fall apart. Others may exhibit chronic emotional distress which includes being negative all the time, inconsistent in their behavior, and/or holds grudges. Unfortunately there is no magic formula or pill for these people to change from low to high EQ.

So what is a leader supposed to do? The first step is to delicately converse with the low EQ person about what is being observed amongst the team members and to collaboratively devise solutions to rectify the situation. It is a good idea to have an objective third person present (human resources, coach, or senior executive) to steer the conversation in a positive manner but also to be a witness to the reactions of the employee. If it is agreed upon that the person needs some assistance, the leader should handle this as quickly as possible. If it gets delayed, the employee could be less trusting of the leader and more problems could occur. If the employee resists taking action, it is then up to the leader to suggest a few alternatives - layoff, reassigning to another department, or suggesting other courses of action outside the workplace i.e. classes or therapy.

EQ is hard to detect during the interview process so leaders should consider different means to identify a candidate's EQ. Reference checks only go so far because the references may be fearful of lawsuits or other means of retaliation. Assessments and testing are helpful but are time-consuming and expensive.

Multiple interviews over a period of time are a smart move because the interviewers can see if the candidate demonstrates consistent behavior. Ideally a combination of all of these should ensure that the final candidate has a high EQ.

Leadership involves dealing with people. Some folks are extroverts and some are introverts. The extroverts feel comfortable around social functions and in dealing with groups almost all the time. On the other hand, introverts tend to be shy and to focus more on individual interactions. Yet, being an extrovert is not an indication of emotional intelligence. Introverts can also show emotional intelligence or what has become commonly called as EQ. What exactly is this EQ? It simply means the capacity, skill and ability to manage one's emotions in relation to other people. Have you ever heard of the quote "people won't care about what you know until they know you care"? That is very true. People care less for knowledge than for emotional connection. And if you are able to connect emotionally to more people, you become a more successful salesperson, businessman or a leader.

Adolf Hitler, Winston Churchill and Barack Obama managed to connect emotionally with people and that is why they became very popular in their respective countries. Connecting emotionally is just one side of the coin. The other side is leadership. Emotional intelligence and transformational leadership go together. One of the tenets of transformational leadership is motivation and idealism. When you appeal to the values of people and to what they hold dear, you can easily sway them to your cause and make you popular. When you are able to do that, you can then sell your transformational agenda to them.

This is not an easy path to take. If you fail in engaging people emotionally, you will be exposed as a fraud and you can easily lose your integrity and your ability to influence people. But if you manage to balance them, you will be able to become an effective leader.

How Emotional Intelligence Helps You Become A Flexible Leader

Emotionally intelligent (EQ) leaders are flexible in adapting their leadership style to those they choose to lead. You will influence and engage employees by being socially savvy regarding which leadership style would be the most appropriate with certain personalities and in specific situations.

The Blanchard and Hersey Model of Leadership

As a leadership model, the best known example was developed by Ken Blanchard, the management guru who later became famous for his One Minute Manager series, and Paul Hersey. They created a model of situational leadership in the late 1960s that allows one to analyze the needs of the situation, and then adopt the most appropriate leadership style. The model has two fundamental concepts; leadership style, and development level.

Leadership Styles:

Blanchard and Hersey characterized leadership style in terms of the amount of direction and support that the leader provides to his or her followers. They categorized all leadership styles into four behavior types, which they named S1 to S4:

S1: Directing Leaders define the roles and tasks of the follower, and supervise them closely. Decisions are made by the leader and announced, so communication is largely one-way.

S2: Coaching Leaders still define roles and tasks, but seeks ideas and suggestions from the follower. Decisions remain the prerogative of the leader, but communication is much more two-way.

S3: Supporting Leaders pass day-to-day decisions, such as task allocation and processes, to the follower. The leader facilitates and takes part in decisions, but control is with the follower.

S4: Delegating Leaders are still involved in decisions and problem-solving, but control is with the follower. The follower decides when and how the leader will be involved.

No one style is considered optimal or desired for all leaders to possess. Effective leaders need to be flexible, and must adapt themselves according to the situation. However, each leader tends to have a natural style, and in applying Situational Leadership he/she must know his/her intrinsic style.

Development Levels:

The right leadership style will depend on the person being led - the follower. Blanchard and Hersey extended their model to include the Development Level of the follower. They stated that the chosen style of the leader should be based on the competence and commitment of his/her followers. They categorized the possible development of followers into four levels, which they named D1 to D4:

D1: Low Competence, High Commitment - They generally lack the specific skills required for the job in hand, however, they are eager to learn and willing to take direction.

D2: Some Competence, Low Commitment - They may have some relevant skills, but will not be able to do the job without help. The task or the situation may be new to them.

D3: High Competence, Variable Commitment - They are experienced and capable, but may lack the confidence to go it alone, or the motivation to do it well or quickly.

D4: High Competence, High Commitment - They are experienced at the job, and comfortable with their own ability to do it well. They may even be more skilled than the leader.

Development Levels are also situational. You might be generally skilled, confident and motivated your job, but would still drop into Level D1 when faced with a task requiring skills you do not possess. For example, many managers are D4 when dealing with the day-to-day running of their department, but move to D1 or D2 when dealing with a sensitive employee issue.

Leadership Development Matching:

Blanchard and Hersey indicate that the leadership style (S1 - S4) of the leader must correspond to the development level (D1 - D4) of the follower. In addition, it is the leader who must adapt, not the follower. To get the most of situational leadership, a leader should be trained in how to operate effectively in various leadership styles, and how to determine the development level of others.

What are your ideas and experiences related to situational leadership? You and your company leaders might from working with an executive coach as part of an emotional intelligence-based leadership development program.

Emotional intelligence in work place

Intelligence is the psychological feature or functioning of a human being's mind and it is being measured by IQ (intelligence quotient). But IQ alone is not the only determinant of a person's ability to get used and adapt with the complex situations of life and his work place efficiency. Intelligence based on emotions can be a factor for determining the success of a person at a work place or outside the work environment. Possessing a good IQ can help decide if you get hired, and EQ gets you fired or promoted. These two skills are common traits you'll find in high flying achievers globally and a combination of both determines the professional success. There is a very close linkage between an individual's intrapersonal function and his interpersonal skills. Here are examples called the 3 R's Concept.

1. RECOGNIZE

2. REDIRECT

3. REFLECT

Recognizing one's own feelings and redirecting those feelings (intrapersonal capacity) and reflecting that redirection of feelings in one's behavior for better communication, effectiveness in interactions and exhibiting greater understanding of one's environment. While human beings are able to relate on a more rational and emotional levels, emotions are the center of our energy, they are the power house of our life. An employee's emotional reaction and their work performance the pendulum has now swung towards recognition that employee emotions are unavoidable and they influence their work behavior and outcomes. The notion that emotions influences work performances are not a strange discovery, what is new that we have found a way to linking emotions to efficiency in work performance and its valuable consequences in organizations.

Your organization is made of people, processes, and property. For a long time, "common wisdom" has been that returns come from investing in the latter two. Yet, in the last decades, new research has challenged that assumption and is increasingly proving that a company's people are the differentiating factor.

In fact, for most businesses, products and property yield little competitive advantage. You develop a new process, and in a week your competitor replicates it. You increase efficiency and lower product cost, and next month a better version is being produced more cheaply in another country. You invest in specialized equipment - and so does the guy down the street.

So where can today's businesses find competitive advantage? With a mobile workforce, globalization, and on-demand information, products and property are not enough. Exceptional organizations are investing in their relationships with customers, employees, and leaders - and over the next decades the people side will increasingly become the only meaningful competitive advantage. If emotional intelligence helps build customer and employee loyalty, helps people innovate and perform, helps leaders build value, then these competencies are essential for world-class performance.

Emotional intelligence affects employee performance in multiple avenues. The employee's own EQ, the interaction between the employee, and the emotional tone - or climate - all significantly affect the way employees feel about work, and the effectiveness of the work they do.

Emotionally Attractive Leaders Create Lovable Companies

If you pause to ponder about the best work you've ever delivered, you'll probably realize you didn't do it all for yourself; you did it for that adorable boss or some other endearing leader who has been your hero in all aspects.

Recall the number of times you may have reached home aglow with a feeling of elation, reliving a positive encounter with an upbeat and supportive boss, perhaps savouring a lighter moment with him or a witty remark about your performance. The bounce that you feel, and the eagerness to get back to office to offer your very best, the 'Thank God It's Monday' phenomenon and the Friday Blues; that's the "afterglow" that lingers and gives you renewed energy to be more productive, and to bring your finest talents to work.

Inspiration is at the core of efficiency and employees react and respond best to leaders who exude warmth, and authentically invest time and effort to connect with them.

In today's global market place most powerful way to influence--and lead--is to be lovable.

The leaders control the switch that can alter the intensity of engagement of the employees of their organization. A leader's jaunty disposition allegorically oxygenates the blood of followers - it's a transfusion into the arteries of corporate ecosystem.

Studies indicate that since World War II, the human brain has been changing on the emotional front. The amygdala, which coordinates emotions, has grown 0.5 of one percent-that is "physiologically remarkable."

Emotions are infectious and leaders are the "emotional thermostats" of the groups and organisations they lead.

A fine example to consider this would be Military forces. How would an "overwhelmed", "nervous", "irritated", "indecisive" or "inconsistent" commander effect troop morale and vigour? How would he energise and inspire his team to weather all storms and lay down their lives at a single command?

"Indecision," is transmissible." It can become incapacitating and habit-forming in an organization, as people take their cues from the leader's state of mind. We want our leaders to be predictable because there is comfort and safety in consistency. Predictability engenders trust and an impulsive leader elicits anxiety and, in some cases, even fear, both of which negatively affect performance and productivity.

Bosses who are lovable, emotionally attractive and charismatic draw people like a magnet. Their ceaseless energy and eternal optimism, ignites their followers to stretch beyond boundaries and deliver superlative performance. They harbour passion for what they do, and this spills over into their business relationships. They blossom because they love people and people love them. There is an emotional bond between the leader and those led. It is seen that organisations with upbeat, enthusiastic, and cohesive executive team are likely to yield better business results. The study also showed that the longer a company was managed by disjointed executive team that didn't get along well, the poorer its image and market returns.

Among the most admired leaders across the world, the following names have stood out owing to their charisma, ability to build a powerful emotional connection with their followers, and communication that inspired and electrified their audiences.

Winston Churchill, Steve Jobs, Mahatma Gandhi, Nelson Mandela, Jack Welch, Abraham Lincoln, Margaret Thatcher, Ronald Reagan, John F Kenned, Bill Clinton, Napoleon Bonaparte

Those with a strong vision were most admired, but motivational, caring, innovative, persistent and ethical qualities were also held in high regard.

For example, John F. Kennedy personified emotionally attractive leadership even before the concept was popularized. Self-awareness, spirited intelligence, self-will, image discipline, empathy and savvy connection to communication, audiences and relationships made him an adorable public figure.

An inspiring speaker, he related to the masses and connected with them on relevant issues. Genuinely likable, when JFK spoke, audiences wanted to concur with him. His tone, poise and deportment communicated credibility and responsibility. He declared a new re-awakening for America and political Washington... people believed. When he was assassinated, a bit of everyone was extinguished.

For charismatic leadership like his, the right blend of emotional intelligence and magnetic charm causes spectacular upshots. It sets the tone, connection and rapport to energize teams to higher levels of synergy and superior achievement. Organizations that cultivate emotional intelligence at the leadership levels experience high levels of team engagement, support for a wide array of initiatives, and a focus on excellence.

The law of reciprocity states that people will reciprocate emotional experiences. Sometimes they reciprocate in a direct reflection (back at you) and other times they reciprocate in an indirect defection (at the next Customer, a coworker or family member).

Research shows that up to 30% of a company's financial results (as measured by key business performance indicators such as revenue growth, return on sales, efficiency and profitability) are determined by the climate of the organization.

Roughly 50-70% of how employees perceive their organization's climate is attributable to the actions and behaviours of their leader. A leader constructs the ecosystem that determines people's moods at the office and their mood, in turn, affects their productivity and level of engagement.. In an organisation people continuously spread their own moods and are impacted by others' moods. When they work in groups, they literally can catch each others' emotions like viruses, a phenomenon known as emotional contagion.

Because employees pay great attention to their leaders' emotions, leaders can strongly influence the mood, and thus attitudes and performance, of their teams through emotional contagion.

There is significant research showing how emotions influence memory, perception and cognition. These factors influence every aspect of an employee's performance - in fact - what is "performance" other than the combination of thought, feeling and behavior?

The varied moods set off a chain reaction: A cranky and ruthless boss creates a toxic organisation filled with negative dark horses who ignore opportunities; an inspirational, inclusive leader generates acolytes for whom any challenge is surmountable. The final link in the chain is performance: profit or loss.

Good moods fire up good performance. The most effective executives display moods and behaviors that are relevant to the prevailing situation, with a healthy blend of optimism. They not only understand and appreciate how other people are feeling - even if it is blue or overwhelmed; but they also exemplify what it looks like to move ahead with hope and humor." The golden trio here is - 'optimism', 'hope' and 'humor'.

But in today's leadership environment, the stress is ever-present. Therefore if you want to be successful over time while maintaining your equilibrium, you have to develop a new skill... emotional talent." Be emotionally attractive. Your emotional attractiveness is directly proportional to your 'likability factor' and translates into how well you consistently produce "positive emotional experiences" in the lives of others, including your staff, prospects and clients.

A word of caution here - In order to be perceived as upbeat and reliable, the leaders cannot be putting on a game face every day. People are very sensitive and can easily see through strained or fake cheerfulness and inconsistent decisions. Leaders cannot sustain their effectiveness if they cannot sustain themselves.

It is required that an executive ascertains, through reflective analysis, how his emotional leadership drives the moods and actions of the organization, and modifies his conduct correspondingly.

How to elevate your emotional attractiveness quotient:

1. Establish Consistent Friendliness - Friendliness is a communication event. It's important for your people to perceive you as friendly. Over time uniformity in behaviour counts far more than first impressions.

2. Relevance is the extent to which a person is able to connect his or her interests, wants, and needs to another's "sweet spot." Mutual interests establish a higher level of relevance. You can accomplish more by developing interest in people than you will in trying to get others interested in you.

a. Identify your frequent contact circle

b. Connect with others' interests

c. Connect with others' wants and needs

3. Empathy is the ability to accurately perceive and comprehend another person's internal frame of reference. It is based upon deep listening and the ability to pick up on more than words.

a. Show an interest in how others feel

b. Experience others' feelings

c. Respond to others' feelings

4. Realness is capability to be genuine and true. It is impossible to have a high EAQ without being genuine, true, and authentic. People who are authentic inspire trust and make others feel good about themselves. They have a strong sense of who they and what they value.

With an ever-expanding marketplace and increasing competition, possessing a high EA factor can be the one thing that distinguishes your business organisation from many others in the race, and can spell the difference between success and failure. It is about enhancing relationships at workplace, which will lead to more effective communication, increased cooperation, satisfied employees, and delighted customers and, ultimately, drive success of your teams and organisations.

LEADERSHIP LIFESTYLE TO EMULATE

Many organizations are aware of the value of emotional intelligence to a leader's success, but uncertain about how to apply it. To gain the full benefit of EI in a leadership role, companies needed to better understand how to best grow EI among leaders.

Correlating leadership styles with emotional intelligence strengths makes it easier for organizations to identify different emotional styles among their leaders/managers and as a result place them in roles calling for their strengths. Because emotional intelligence is a skill and it's very easy to learn, companies can provide training and support for leaders who need to modify their leadership style to be more effective.

Leadership styles are often determined by the leader's emotional strengths, often expressed in four or five distinct clusters of emotional strengths: Self-Perception, Self-Expression, Interpersonal, Decision Making and Stress Management.

These 5 clusters also reflect five different leadership styles and much is gained by naming them in more commonly used terms i.e.: The Star, The Coach, The

Social Worker, The Engineer, and The Physician makes it easier for everyone to comprehend the differences. The necessary skills among the 5 clusters are the same but the names have changed. A "Star" styled leader, for instance, is likely to call upon his/her self-awareness and self-confidence to lead while a "Physician" style leader is likely to leverage their ability to manage stress and "role with the punches" to manage. A "Coach" styled leader is often engaged in making certain their direct reports understand the rules and strategize for victory, while a "Social Worker" styled leader is always focused on others and attempting to achieve goals through other by better understanding them. Finally, the "Engineer" is all about tasks and problem solving and creating realistic objectives.

Of course, each of these leadership styles is shaped by their understanding and natural abilities but determining the style most needed for the task and finding a leader with the necessary style, has just become a lot easier. Now organizations can ask and scientifically identify the leadership style that matches the needs of the job. For example, what kind of task would likely require a "Star" type leader?

Tasks that require "Star" type leaders are those jobs what have ambitious objectives, requiring a positive attitude and ability to motivate others would be a simple description. What type of leader could best head-up a large public project, for instance? The "Social Worker" leader might be good fit here since he/she is likely highly skilled at connecting with people and sensitive to the needs of others.

This subject really requires much more space and time than we can give it here, but I am betting that you are beginning to get the picture. The picture of how results can be improved by matching Emotional Leadership Styles with the needs of the job and how many profits can be advanced by doing so.

In organizations the skills needed for SELF can be grouped into self-awareness (emotional awareness, accurate self-assessment, self-confidence) and SELF MANAGEMENT (self-control, transparency, adaptability, achievement, initiative, optimism). Other social awareness skill are social awareness (empathy, organizational awareness) and RELATIONSHIP MANAGEMENT (inspiration, influence, developing others, change catalyst, conflict management, teamwork and collaboration).

In the course of this book we have discussed and talked about self-management, self-awareness and empathy, it would be reasonable that this time we can talk about work place relationship in terms of relationship as a social awareness skill.

Relationship Management

The management of relationship has been a facet of business for as long as business transactions have existed. On the most basic level, Relationship Management is about interaction with customers. From a broader perspective one can consider employees, suppliers and consumers as customers, the employees being the internal customers of the organization. Relationship Management deals with the treatment and management of partnerships, connections, linkages and chains between business entities.

For the purposes of this paper, we view Relationship Management (RM) as a conscious and planned activity. It would be misleading to suggest that there have not been relationships in business or any focus on relationships by companies. However, the thrust of RM, as expounded in recent times, points to a more tactical and strategic approach to focusing on the customer rather than a relentless focus on the competition.

After the economic downturn of the 90s, many companies started to examine the possible benefits to be gained from less negotiation strong-arming, closeness to suppliers and the establishment of constructive relationships with strategic stakeholders. This does not suggest that RM was founded in the US, or has not existed before then; the Japanese had perfected RM and value-concretization into an art form on the basis of social structure and communal creed.

RM itself has not just many types but many levels. The manufacturer has his suppliers and the end users as his customers; the retailer has the manufacturers and the end users as his customers, and manufacturer, the supplier and every organization with a tactical or strategic agenda have internal customers.

Different types of RM have been identified, ranging from the transactional, the collaborative and the formation of alliances, which is also known as partnerships or value-added exchanges. The alliance is a partnership with suppliers that involves a mutual beneficiary arrangement where cost-cutting ventures are jointly addressed by both buyer and seller, the seller being considered an extension of the buyer's organization. The business relationship between Japanese suppliers using JIT is a good example. For example Toyota holds a strong alliance even with its 3rd tier vendors. The result of such partnerships means added value, reduced production and transport costs, a more seamless supply and delivery network, and maintenance of exceptional quality, as per TQM considerations.

Traditionally, companies were preoccupied with rigorous competition, firm-induced and firm-controlled business strategies, focus on short-term profits and strategies and independent decision-making. This transactional existence meant a focus more on the competition than the customer, a concentration on short-term profits rather than long-term strategic gains and likelihood to be blind to opportunities for expansion and change. Today's strategically-minded companies are pre-occupied with partnership with other firms, collaboration and coaction, boundarylessness, joint decision-making and a focus on long term benefits. With today's business climate, one can easily foresee a rapidly changing business environment where manufacturers will have the most fruitful partnerships with every member of the supply chain and the consumers, a scenario where the manufacturer will run a 'virtual factory' with the effective and efficient use of value chain networks unlimited by geographical location or consideration.

RM functions on a strategic, a tactical and an operational level. Businesses that are product-oriented ensure effective performance of their products, in the design, the features and output; the production-oriented business (not to be confused with the product-oriented) believe in mass production at a cheap scale on the notion that the customer uses low-price as a singular consideration; sales-oriented businesses put a lot of stock in advertising, promotions and public relations while the customer-centric enterprise strives to understand its customers preferences and purchasing behavior and models its business activities to suit this. This is considered strategic RM. The operational level deals with automating the customer management process using computer applications and devices across market, sales force and service categories. Tactical RM deals with using the data from customer management computer applications to add value both to the customer and the company.

While it would be immensely useful to run a customer database to keep the organization in sync with full information with its customers, RM especially from a strategic perspective delves deeper than mere software; it deals with a 'pull' strategy, letting the wants and needs of the customer dictate what products and services are offered, rather than the other way round, using a production-oriented strategy to 'push' products and services that the consumers may or may not need, but which does not ultimately satisfy the customer.

Companies generate more revenue when they satisfy - and because of this retain- their customers. It is hereby propounded that the simple economic fact that customer retention is cheaper than customer attraction provides the customer with an intrinsic importance to business performance than anything else.

Relationship management: The final area you need to develop in raising your EQ is that of relationship management. We can look upon this trait in connection with your profession. This is the aspect of your EQ that enables you to succeed in inspiring other people and helping them to reach their full potential. It is also vital in negotiating successfully, resolving conflicts and working with others toward a shared goal. Your success in this final area is directly correlated to your success in the other three areas because management is all about successfully interacting with other people. At the end of the day isn't efficient management all about getting the work done?

LOW EMOTIONAL CAPABILITIES CAN RUIN YOU

Some time ago I observed at the place where I work that employees having low emotional competencies tend to lose their jobs even after being selected from hundreds of applicants who were interviewed. There was this employee joined the organization, during the faculty development programme was called to share her experiences but she refused by saying that she is not prepared, our director took her refusal as her shyness, nervousness to come in front and gave so much motivating examples from his own life and with expressing his disappointment due to her refusal and then again asked her to speak but all in vain because she took that behavior as insult failing to recognize her emotions and emotional responses and those of director's and reacted as a slave of emotions. She could not bear that incidence and never came back.

Emotional intelligence can help explain why employees with strong academic backgrounds or cognitive skills are not always the best team members and leaders. Emotional Intelligence shapes human behavior in diverse realms including workplace, community and schools. On the individual plane, it is found to relate to work performance, our ability to communicate effectively, build meaningful interpersonal relationships, resolve everyday problems, scholastic achievement, and even our potential to make moral decisions. Admitting the possibility of EI to amplify our understanding of how individuals behave and adjust to their social environment, it forms an area of immediate attention to HR managers and practitioners.

Bad emotional experience always takes its toll in terms of thwarted problem-solving ability, innovation, commitment, creativity and productivity. Diversity in appearance, food habits, beliefs, thought patterns, reactions, choices and so on define any and every workplace. Nothing could be easier to handle this except by honoring it. HR people need to ensure that staffers have means to express their varied beliefs and opinions. To encourage and stimulate healthy emotional climate among employees, HR managers should:

1) Promote open communication and honest feedback.

2) Emphasize that speaking about emotion within organization is fine.

3) Specify that loud thinking among team members is okay.

4) Enlighten staffers that it is no sin to admit some of management's ideas may be flawed.

5) Organize standardized training on Emotional Intelligence and competency building.

6) Stress the value of striking emotional bonds with one's allotted task.

7) Highlight the benefits of maintaining informal, cheerful and positive work spaces.

Emotional intelligence is supposed to factor as a crucial recruitment criterion along with other relevant technical skills or business knowledge. It should be considered or should be used for the recruitments of fresh staffs into organsations. In case of promotions and succession planning, EI should figure as a decisive factor, mainly if leadership roles are foreseen. Even while selecting and grooming people with good potential EI should be emphasized. Similarly training and development programs must spotlight EI. Through some emotional release session or team-building exercises, the fact is, today, more and more CEO's are passing on the mantle of responsibility as counselors to their workforce. The biggest imperative before all the leaders and business owners is to make sure that negative emotions do not end up creating negative spaces and negative consequences within organizations. Unleashing a culture of positivity and openness holds the key to effective emotion management in any company.

EI FOR THE SALESMAN

EQ enables you to maximize your own sales potential by firstly understanding yourself and then understanding how other people are made up - enabling you to communicate in a way that they would like, rather than from your point of view.

Emotional Intelligence is known as EQ which for the dyslexic people out there (of which I am one) does cause some confusion but highlights the recognition that EQ and IQ are similar; one is a measure of intelligence and the other a measure of the emotions.

Emotional Intelligence is more important than IQ.

Research shows that EQ in a commercial environment may actually be significantly more important than information processing abilities and technical expertise combined. In fact, some studies indicate that EQ is more than twice as important as standard IQ abilities. Furthermore, evidence increasingly shows that the higher one goes in an organization, the more important EQ can be. For those in leadership positions, Emotional Intelligence skills are believed to account for close to 90 percent of what distinguishes outstanding leaders from those judged as average. IQ gets you hired, but EQ gets you promoted.

So what makes a great sales person and can EQ help?

I am sure you have heard many times people referring to someone as 'a natural'. Or that someone can 'sell fridges to Eskimos'. These sales people have great people skills or EQ; they are in tune with peoples' emotions, body language and can read people. It's a gift. Like playing great golf.

I can remember when I was working in presales on an account. When we finished the presentation the sales guy said to me:

"That went well, don't you think?"

Went well!?! It was terrible, people were looking at their watches, there were no questions, and we really had not understood the client's issues as we spent most of the time telling them how great we were. I could not understand how he could have come away from the same presentation with such a different point of view. We were clearly in trouble, and needed to do some serious rethinking if we were going to win the account.

The difference between the sales guy and me was in gauging how the pitch went. He had not tuned in to the unspoken signals that the people in the room were giving out.

Almost everyone at a pitch will be polite and tell you the meeting was a positive one, and that they can see good things ahead, but is this verbal reassurance backed up by the other signals they give out? If you can't pick up on these signals - you won't win many accounts, and sales will be a short career.

Emotional Intelligence Decreases Workplace Stress

Social Responsibility

At work, as in relationships, you have certain choices you can make. You can act like a mature, thoughtful, empathic, and responsible person or you can indulge what Freud called in his personality theory the id. This nasty little piece of who we are was described by Freud as blind, instinctual, irrational strivings. If you give in to your id responses, you will show very little social responsibility and you will become an aggravating and difficult colleague. Being prepared to give and take, to understand the other person's point of view, to maintain perspective and keep a larger view, and be generous in your relationships with others will increase harmony and decrease workplace stress for you and your colleagues.

Interpersonal Relationships

It's not unrealistic to say that there two types of people in this world - the givers and the takers. When I'm involved in marriage counseling I do a quick assessment to see which end of the spectrum is the chief personal style of each partner. Obviously, if you have two takers and no compromise you will have a marital battleground where each partner slugs away to get as much they can from the other. If you have a giver and taker then you will find one person whose life opportunities are sacrificed to the selfish interests of the other. When you have two givers, you'll probably have a comfortable, generous, caring, reciprocal sharing relationship - you know you are on a winner. In many ways, you can see the same system operating in the workplace with some people fighting tooth and nail to win at every opportunity. Developing collaborative teams requires people to be sensitive and committed to building positive, respectful, sharing relationships. When these relationships are the dominant interpersonal characteristics of work teams everyone's workplace stress is reduced.

Stress Tolerance

Everyone has a different capacity to deal with stress and anxiety. Some people have, as they say, a short fuse and are unable to tolerate even the smallest amount of stress. This is a pain and misery to everyone around them who has to put up with their limited capacity to manage stress. We can improve our capacity to deal proactively and effectively with stress; we can increase our stress tolerance mechanisms. This requires us to be mature and thoughtful and not indulge ourselves in juvenile expressions of frustration and impatience.

Impulse Control

One of my research areas is ADHD and a key characteristic of some people with ADHD is a diminished capacity for impulse control and self-regulatory management. Unfortunately, there are too many people in the workplace who show a reckless disregard for even a small amount of impulse control. They seem to believe that they have an incontestable right to vent their emotional eruptions whenever they feel like it and without regard to others. The converse of this is the responsible person who doesn't elevate other people's stress levels but carefully and effectively deals with the pressures and stress that they are experiencing.

This is probably a little too technical and I certainly have glossed over some of the complexities of each of these personal styles but these are complex matters. I could have given a simple tip checklist to reduce workplace stress based on emotional intelligence but this wouldn't be fair to either the interested reader of this fascinating area of personality and cognitive theory. My message is fairly simple - if you want to manage personal stress and reduce workplace stress you have a responsibility to behave in a mature, emotionally intelligent way. Of course I know the response most people would make - I'm not the problem, it's my colleague who has very low emotional intelligence and creates all the stress in this organization. Well, let's begin as they say - physician heals thyself. Then, after ensuring that you are OK, work to develop behaviors that reflect emotionally intelligent groups. I agree with the Harvard research that highly skilled work teams do reflect high group emotional intelligence and are much more productive. I'm also certain that people lucky enough be working in groups with high emotional intelligence and strong interpersonal responsibility have much lower personal stress levels and cope much more effectively with workplace stress.

Some real life examples of the benefit of developing emotional intelligence in the workplace include:

1. Greater sales

A study of over 40 Fortune 500 companies revealed that sales people with high emotional intelligence out performed those with medium to low EI by 50%.

2. Greater productivity

That same study revealed that technical programmers who were measured in the top 10% of the emotional intelligence competencies were cranking out new software three times faster than those with lower measurements. Even more astounding, a Dallas based company who underwent measuring its entire staff determined that employees with a high EI were 20 times more productive than those with a lower score.

3. Stability of staff

Another Fortune 500 had been using personality assessment for years in an attempt to slow down turn over in its high turnover sales force with little success. By implementing EI assessments, and including EI topics like stress management, self-awareness and social skills, they were able to stop the brain drain and increase retention by 67%. The firm calculated it saved over $30 million by reducing recruiting and training costs and increasing sales through retention.

4. Worker satisfaction

A Midwest community bank was forced to cut staff by 30% due to the tough economic times we have experienced recently. The remaining staff was evaluated for their emotional intelligence which resulted in certain changes in organizational structure. People were assigned positions where there EI was best suited for the task. The result is the bank now produces more with fewer people because the fewer people are now better suited for their positions and find them more fulfilling.

5. Improved risk management

Two studies, one for retail operations and one involving the construction industry determined that there was a correlation between low emotional intelligence and theft or shrinkage. In addition, persons with a low emotional intelligence score were more likely to have accidents on the job.

6. Amazing customer service

A luxury car dealership whose entizre marketing plan was built on customer experience and customer service was expanding and wanted to make sure they hired the best customer oriented employees to staff the new facility. The dealership utilized an EI assessment test and EI interviewing techniques that were designed to uncover a high level of empathy in candidates. This process was used to select everyone from the GM down to the valet. One year after opening, the new dealership was rated in the top 10% of the auto companies 200 plus dealers for both sales and customer satisfaction.

7. Better organizational communication

A Towers Watson study of both U.S. and Canadian firms disclosed that companies who do a better job of communicating with their employees outperform those who do not financially. On average a company with an exceptional communications program delivered a 47%

greater return to shareholders than the least communicative firms.

Could your organization benefit from assessing your staff's emotional intelligence? Can you see how including EI in training and personal development programs can help the bottom line? As a professional, you owe it to yourself to at least investigate the possibilities.

8. When a team is created it will create an environment of social interdependence and that can be a good thing or bad depending on how it is managed. If the team leader explains that the group will focus on team goals and requires the input of all team members to be successful, the result is a greater effort to collaborate. However if the team is set up as competitors ie "the first one to sell 100 widgets gets a big bonus' then you have a team that consists of individuals with individual goals.

9. EI and team work

Positive and effective relationships between team members have been demonstrated to be the superior emotional setting to drive results. Members who share a bond both professionally and personally will work harder to achieve success for those for the group than a team where those relationships have not been developed. Developing emotional intelligence through exercises and training can greatly improve the odds of effective team performance.

If you are a team manager you really set the tone. If you want the most out of your team, work to set an environment that develops the relationships not tears them down through competition

12 ELEMENTS OF EMOTIONAL INTELLIGENCE

Intellect can be measured by standardized IQ tests but there is no actual measure of the "EQ," or Emotional Quotient. Even without a test, it's obvious when someone has a high IQ and it's just as obvious when someone has a high EQ. Rather than try to measure it, though, it's more useful to look at the various elements that go into emotional intelligence.

While the IQ remains stable over a person's lifetime, the EQ can be developed. Acquiring and practicing the following elements will enable you to boost your EQ.

The first element of emotional intelligence is empathy. The ability to understand what other people are feeling will make you more sensitive and aware and will result in more meaningful relationships.

The second element is the recognition that your actions have consequences. This understanding will enable you to make conscious choices in your life and to avoid unnecessary difficulties.

Third on the list is good judgment. The gift of making well-thought-out decisions and seeing people for who they really are will maximize the possibilities of success in all areas of your life.

Number four is personal responsibility. When you hold yourself accountable and don't blame anyone else for your mistakes or misfortunes, you are empowered to change things for the better. Other people respect you, because you own up to your part in your relationships.

The fifth element is insight. The ability to see yourself clearly and to understand your own motivations allows for the possibility of personal growth. Insight into others allows you to have a greater impact in your relationships.

Element number six is mental flexibility. Being able to change your mind or to see things from different points of view makes it possible for you to navigate all sorts of relationships and to succeed where other, more rigid thinkers would fail.

The seventh element is compassion. Being honest with yourself can be painful but with a kind and gentle attitude, it's much easier. This type of compassion facilitates personal transformation, while compassion toward others supports deeper, more loving connections.

The eighth element is integrity. Following through on commitments and keeping your promises creates much good-will in personal and professional relationships and promotes success in both arenas.

Ninth on the list is impulse control. Thinking before speaking or acting gives you a chance to make deliberate, even sophisticated choices about how you present yourself to others. Not acting out of primitive impulses, urges or emotions avoids social embarrassment.

The tenth element is the ability to defer gratification. It's one thing to want something but the ability to put off having it is empowering. Mastery of your needs allows you to to prioritize around life goals.

Number eleven on the list is perseverance. Sticking with something, especially when it's challenging, allows you to see it through to completion and demonstrates to others that you are dependable and potentially a high achiever.

The twelfth and final element is courage. Emotional courage (as opposed to the physical variety) is the ability to do the right thing, see the truth, open your heart and trust yourself and others enough to be vulnerable, even if all this is frightening. This causes others to hold you in high regard.

All these elements combine within you to make up your emotional intelligence. With a high EQ, even a simple person is at an advantage in life. Without it, even someone with the most brilliant intellect is at a disadvantage.

EMOTIONAL INTELLIGENCE IN THE HOME: RAISING EMOTIONALLY INTELLIGENT CHILDREN

Parents need to be emotionally intelligent to have any influence on teens which will allow them to become socially conscious while remaining stable and flexible in their emotions.

When a parent interacts with a child, especially a teenager, certain stress levels are brought in. The parent needs to keep this stress under control as this can be easily perceived by the teenager. This stress could lead to the child finding interaction constantly irksome and could cause the child to avoid the situation where he has to talk to people, basically this is why certain kids are extremely shy and avoid social life. Accept the fact that as a parent you are also a human and have your own needs of time and space. Let the teenager know this firmly enough and it is almost sure that the teen will accept the fact and live with it. Be consistent in all your dealings with their problems and even if they find your decisions irksome, they will still respect it for the constancy that you show.

Let not any feeling of guilt come into any dealings with your teenager. Children are always quick to spot such feelings and more than likely to take advantage of it. If you are feeling guilty in any way, better to correct the situation that has caused this guilt. Show your children the respect that his fledgling and developing personality has come to expect. Listen to their problems and the suggestions that they have and never lay down the law. Explain your situation in an adult manner. Teenagers will respond when you put the onus of understanding on them.

Emotional resilience learned early in life assists in recovering from misfortunes and disappointments, thus fostering emotional health. Teaching your child to be emotionally resilient will help him/her be in control and build confidence to work through challenging situations effectively. Becoming emotionally resilient in childhood will provide a basic foundation for your child's emotional health in adolescence and adulthood. Emotions shape your child's interactions with others and affect his or her behaviors resulting from those interactions. In order to avoid conflict, or address situations adequately when it arises, your child should learn to understand his or her feelings, be able to identify them, and regulate them. It is important to teach children there is a whole gamut of emotions that can be expressed in various ways. However, knowing how to express them in a meaningful way will help your child in solving social conflicts and maintaining relationships. One way of promoting development of emotional competence is to help your child develop vocabulary that expresses feelings. Parents can also assist their children in recognizing various emotions and teaching them that emotions can be changed by their thinking.

Emotions are driven by behaviors. However, children must learn that emotions should not take control over their actions. It is crucial for children to know that expressing feelings helps in preventing and resolving problems. They need to be taught that bottled-up feelings lead to misunderstandings, anxiety, anger, and depression.

When your child does not express emotions, he or she is more likely to experience angry outbursts that might come from being sad, embarrassed, or frustrated. Perhaps, your child feels guilty about something he or she did, is afraid, or feels helpless and chooses to express those negative feelings of emotional stress with angry outbursts. This inability to deal with stress in a constructive way most of the time stems from the lack of understanding one's own emotions, emotions of others, and lacking the ability to express feelings effectively.

Signs of Emotional Fragility

- ✓ Regression of behaviors
- ✓ Withdrawal

- ✓ Excessive clinginess
- ✓ Bedwetting
- ✓ Nightmares
- ✓ Aggression

One of the most important things a parent can do to foster a child's healthy emotional development is to promote positive family communication. That includes positive reinforcement, which is praising your child for positive behaviors, giving encouragement, and avoidance of negative criticism when expected outcomes are not achieved. Also, providing consistency is extremely important for a child's emotional health, as it aids in avoiding ambiguity and uncertainty. If a child knows what's expected of him or her, they will most likely comply, thus avoiding frustration, anger, and possibly humiliation.

Younger children might be more open and willing to express their feelings. In adolescence, family communication might become more challenging as the teen tries to suppress their feelings in an attempt to resolve them alone. Parenting teenagers requires patience and the ability to be supportive. Frequently, conversation with your teen at home might be extremely difficult. However, your teen may try to open up while riding with you in a car where there is no eye contact, thus the confrontation seems to be less intimidating. Building a sound foundation of emotional resilience in childhood will help your adolescent achieve emotional health. Should getting through to your child become impossible, or he or she become withdrawn and exhibits signs of emotional instability, don't be afraid to seek help.

UNDERSTANDING THE EMOTIONS OF OTHERS

As hard as you may try to understand other people's situation and suffering, you'll not find it easy to relate with unless you go through the same circumstance. You will find it hard to understand their needs but if you are sensitive enough to feel what they feel, I am sure there is no problem expressing your empathy rather than your sympathy. When you put yourself on other people's shoes, you also feel their emotions like being angry, sad, hurt and left out. The ability to be able to predict how other people might feel is a part of emotional intelligence (EQ), a skill we can all improve on with practice. When we understand how other people are likely to react, it can guide our interactions and dealings with them.

By nature, people are extremely self-centered, always thinking about themselves alone and everyone tries to look at a situation from their own perspective, which is a perspective that reflects from the cumulative experiences of their lives, they hardly empathize any situation and try to look at it from the other side. Sometimes we just fail to comprehend the situation because we make decisions quicker than we thought. Our peripheral vision is blurred due to our easy to judge behavior. When we understand other people's feelings, it actually requires a threshold level of empathy to even be aware of what others feel. Most of us are not able to understand other people's feelings. We are too preoccupied with our own shortcomings that we failed to notice that there are still other beings out there who suffered more than we've been through. Though life is a matter of choice; our willingness to listen and understand others predicament can help boosts their morale. This is easier said than done. In reality, we are quick to make assumptions without digging deeper what makes them act or do such foolish actions that made them suffer than satisfied. I can understand that it is really difficult to feel what other people feel because some people are not willing to listen. We just need to regard people not on what they do but what their situation is because when it comes to understanding others, we seldom use our heart. Most often than not, we use our mouth to speak harsh words to others rather than let our emotions speak the truth.

We are more thoughtful when we listen with our hearts than our ears. We need to learn how to accept our mistakes before we can understand the mistakes of others. Most sensible people understand what they do. But it does not mean that they are mean. It just happened that they focused mostly on themselves rather than on other people you will find out that people who frequently have outbursts of anger, depression or flamboyant enthusiasm are generally disapproved of in the early stage of their childhood. There are some children who suffered emotional trauma in their formative years because of parents' neglect. True, we have to be patient in understanding their situation but it doesn't mean that we are going to tolerate such display of inappropriate behavior. If they are not corrected right now, then they will become liabilities of the society than assets.

But never ever assume everything is fine just because someone isn't having a nervous breakdown. We all have our individual problems, angst and upsets in life. We just have to be sensitive with the underlying currents that made them who they are. It gives us an advantage in trying to help. Emphatic understanding is very important especially if we want to know what others have been through.

Although many people have heard of empathy, (psychics who are able to sense or feel the emotions of others), few people fully understand what it means to possess empathic psychic abilities. People naively assume that this ability is a great and wonderful gift, and that it does not come at a cost to the psychic who possesses it. The truth is, this rare talent can also be a deadly burden to bear.

These psychics come with wide ranges of sensitivity. On one end of the spectrum are the emphatic psychics who can only vaguely recognize other people's feelings, while on the other end there are the powerful psychics who feel people's emotions as though they were their own. People who are able to relate with people on an emotional or empathetic level is called an empath, To be a compassionate person, we have to accept the kind of person we are and embrace our good values. The very essence of being compassionate is the eagerness to show empathy, to feel and help others with their suffering. This feeling helps us to generate more positive thoughts, real emotions and acts as a starting point for developing happiness within ourselves. Admittedly, it can be wonderful to be able to understand another person's feelings, and to be able to understand them and to help them cope with their feelings if they need help; empathic psychics are often skilled at emotional healing therapy. This is a process in which the psychic can share the burden of an extreme emotion, thereby lessening the pain that it is causing the patient. Alternatively, a psychic can guide a patient through difficult emotional distress by using their sensitive, intimate understanding of a patient's emotional state of mind.

How Can We Develop A Kind And Compassionate Mind

To develop a kind and compassionate mind it's going to take a lot of practice, but you will find a way to handle it. You can start by feeling compassionate for yourself every day. It might sound uncomfortable to imagine this. But try and say to yourself loudly so you can hear yourself say at any time of your day, make positive words of declaration every day say to yourself "I am a kind and compassionate person". Make it a priority to stay in conducive environment that is quiet, where you are relaxed, pause, slow down and spend at least three minutes every day to take deep breaths and get your head space. Reflect on all the wonderful qualities you would like to have as a person who is kind, loving, compassionate and someone who is full of life. Now, understand each emotion and find an opportunity to express that emotion. Imagine the kind person you are, feel it and do something as an act of kindness. Imagine the loving and compassionate person you are and feel it. See how your thoughts change, how your body reacts, what sensations you feel, how you see the world around you right when you feel these emotions. Take each quality and imagine being a person who thinks feels and act with this quality.

EMOTIONAL INTELLIGENCE AND SELF-ESTEEM

Emotional intelligence (EQ) is about being aware of your emotions. If you have a high emotional intelligence you know what you are feeling from moment to moment, and in most cases you also know why you are feeling as you do. Furthermore, you know what it is that you need to do in order to change your emotions in situations when you wish to feel differently. Emotional intelligence thus makes you more aware of your personal needs and it increases your ability to take good care of yourself. Having a high emotional intelligence cannot be unaccompanied by high self-awareness. Thus, if you have a high EQ you also know yourself well. It is easier to build a high self-esteem (i.e. to develop a good relationship with yourself) when you know yourself. How can you accept and love someone you don't know? For this reason, self-esteem and emotional intelligence go hand in hand. As you raise your emotional intelligence you also learn to understand yourself better, accept yourself (including both negative and positive emotions), satisfy your personal needs and value yourself more. Everything gets easier when you improve the relationship with yourself.

Emotional intelligence is not only about understanding oneself, but also about understanding other people. With a high EQ you can enter a room full of people and immediately get a sense of how the people in that room are feeling at that moment. You can understand other people's needs better, and this makes it easier for you to help them to satisfy those needs. This makes it easier to handle all different kinds of people because you know how to make them feel good. We all have a social need, and as we raise our emotional intelligence we become better at building and keeping relationships that help us satisfy that need. We make ourselves feel better and we raise our self-esteem by helping others feel good.

To raise your emotional intelligence you simply have to listen to yourself more often. Take a break and ask your body what it is feeling. Do you feel some tension or pain anywhere? Listen to your intuition (your gut feeling). As soon as you open up to the information that is already within you, you will find out that you "know" much more than you were aware of before. Do not ignore or try to push emotions away. They have something important to tell you. Your emotions will help you to raise your self-esteem. Many people with low self-esteem try to ignore their negative emotions. They may have learnt through their childhoods that negative emotions are bad and should not be expressed, or they may simply not know how to handle their emotions. People with low self-esteem often translate having negative emotions into being a bad person. They assume that if they are feeling sad, angry or scared it must be because they are either doing something wrong or they do not deserve to feel differently. People with high self-esteem pay attention and are sensitive to their emotions without ignoring them or sweeping them aside. They do not equate feeling bad with being bad. They handle negative feelings in a positive manner. People with high self-esteem learn from their negative emotions and take active steps to make themselves feel better (for example by making sure that they get their unfulfilled needs met).

To keep your self-esteem high you thus have to accept your emotions. Ask yourself what you need in order to heal your wound or to find better balance. If you need social support, ask for it! If you need to slow down and relax, do it! You may simply need to have a good cry to offload some pressure, and everything will be fine again. Welcome your emotions and listen to what they are trying to tell you!

How to Improve Your Emotional Intelligence

1. Identify your own emotion at the time you are exhibiting it or shortly thereafter and name it. (Anger, frustration, joy, grief, abandonment, fear, love, confusion, etc.)

2. Identify what caused the emotion. (Memory from the past, friction with a disrespected colleague, threat of looking bad.)

3. Accept the emotion and what it has meant to your emotional development. (Is there a pattern? Are you perceived as eruptive, self-centered etc.?)

4. Express the named emotion and the cause to whoever is witnessing it or to someone else appropriate. (This may include an apology, an explanation, a compliment, etc.)

If you feel that others have a pre-conceived negative opinion of you, you may ask them how you are being perceived. If you don't want to do that, build your own self-awareness by quickly naming your emotions as they develop, identify what causes them, accepting them and expressing them to someone. Only then will you be able to catch yourself and project in a calmer more collective manner as opposed to exhibiting predictable negative behavior. Decreasing the negative behavior will help to reform opinions from colleagues.

If you are able to identify and control your own emotions with practice, then you are ready to put those skills to use for your team whenever there is a conflict or need for change. For individuals to work together they must build bridges across perspectives with compassion. Compassion is not agreement. It is a consideration for another person's feelings and is essential on teams before two objecting parties' lapse into defensiveness and a toxic work environment ensues.

Emotional Intelligence With Your Colleagues.

1. Ask yourself what you need to stop doing to make the team work effectively.

2. Be curious and compassionate to the others' perspectives. Learn to view things from their angle too. Be a good listener ask questions. Articulate what you understand their point of view to be. Use "I" statements and not "you" statements.

3. Use the steps above to understand the emotions and behaviors of others.

4. Make a suggestion as to how the conflict may be handled with compassion to all parties.

Identify the ideal self, In a way, this is analogous to imagining the future state of an organization - what it would look like without defects, rework, misalignment of work and requirements, etc. - but the ideal self is much more personal. One person's ideal self, building on his or her core identity and aspirations, will be different from another's ideal self. Personal change starts with envisioning the ideal self - the way one would like to be, to work, and to be perceived, but this is much more personal. This has three elements:

Awareness Of One's Strengths

An image of the desired future and a sense of hope that the desired future is attainable Insight into the ideal self are not always straightforward. One might simply extrapolate a trend of the present instead of envisioning a truly desired future self. Talking about aspirations with trusted friends or mentors can help. But identifying a clear picture of the future self-one wishes to be is a foundational step in Intentional Change Theory.

Identify the real self is not as easy as it sounds. In "Primal Leadership" Goleman, Boyatzis, and McKee report, "We found that an alarming number of leaders do not really know if they have resonance with their organizations. Rather they suffer from CEO disease; it's one unpleasant symptom is the sufferer's near-total ignorance about how his mood and actions appear to the organization. It's not that leaders don't care how they are perceived; most do. But they incorrectly assume that they can decipher this information themselves. Worse, they think that if they are having a negative effect, someone will tell them. They're wrong." The greatest challenge is to see oneself as others do. Using multiple sources of feedback can be very useful. Many organizations use 360 reviews for all individuals in management positions. However, the self-assessments are customarily inflated because it is the start of negotiation position. [Boyatzis uses 360 reviews to measure the correlation between EQ and operating results, but he says they throw away the self-assessments as "they are largely delusional."] Identification of the actual self requires honest and objective feedback. Behavioral feedback (such as video) and psychological tests can also help.

Develop a learning agenda, come up with an agenda and plan in contrast to the stream of to-dos and complying with agendas of others, the learning agenda is development focused. In Leadership Development from a Complexity Perspective, Boyatzis says that "a person often needs a type of permission to let go of old habits and try new ones." A learning agenda provides that type of structure for exploration and learning. The fourth step is Experimentation and Practice, look for feedback, and practice again. A consultant, coach or mentor should help the individual who has embarked on intentional change to find safe settings to practice the characteristics of the effective leader he or she envisions. Finally build Helping relationships, someone whose experience you can learn from. People like Coaches, mentors, guides are very helpful to someone aiming to transition to the ideal self through practicing greater EQ and inspirational leadership.

HOW TO USE THE ABCDE THEORY OF EMOTIONS

The ABCDE model is a model that makes it necessary for each stage be completed before advancing to the next stage. During moments of low emotional intelligence the ABCDE model is a useful tool to help employees reach a resolution. Let us take a closer look at each stage of the ABCDE model and how it's been used by coaches to groom people into becoming better emotional beings.

ABCDE Model

A = Activating event

B = Belief system

C = Emotional Consequences of A and B

D = Disputing irrational thoughts and beliefs.

E = Cognitive and Emotional effects of "updated" beliefs

Activating Event/Situation: The activating stage involves a triggering occurrence or situation and coming to terms with the negative feelings and emotions that are related to the event. It is important to look closely at the automatic thoughts - those thoughts that have an immediate reaction to an experience. It is helpful to put down these thoughts and feelings associated with the event in writing. This stage must be completed before moving on to stage

Belief System: the second stage is the belief stage, in this stage a coach guides the employee to recognize that beliefs trigger negative automatic thoughts. This is significant because thoughts ultimately determine the actions that are taken. Beliefs are formed throughout a person's life, from childhood on, and need to be analyzed in order to change those beliefs that cause negative thoughts and actions.

Emotional Consequences: This stage involves discussing the internal and external trait that followed as a result of an employee's beliefs and situation. The internal consequences are those emotions felt inside such as a change in heart rate or stomach butterflies. External consequences are the behaviors exhibited such as yelling at another person or slamming a door when exiting a room. As in all stages, this must be completed before progressing to the next step.

Dispute: In stage 4 thoughts and beliefs now at a disputed to cross check if they are rational or irrational. If they are worth it or not should and must beliefs that seem concrete and do not allow flexibility need to be disputed for validity. For example, if a belief that all employees must be nice to each other is held, during this stage it will be disputed to determine if this belief is true.

When looking at the Dispute stage there are three key kinds of disputes that can be used:

Scientific dispute – Are there any proof to the claims or basis for the belief, feelings, or thought pattern

Functional dispute – Is the belief supporting some other, potentially unconscious goals?

Logical dispute – Does the belief system make common sense? Is there any generalization or other thought pattern influencing these beliefs?

Example: A person who recognizes the thought pattern and changes and sees they are not based on truth or logic and adapts over the time to a view of believing that they can do a better job at expressing his beliefs.

Exchange: In this final stage, beliefs that have been disputed and determined as irrational are exchanged for beliefs that are rational. Replacing negative beliefs that cause negative thoughts is necessary to reframe an employee's thinking for the future. Changing beliefs, thought patterns and actions does not occur over night. But once the new, positive beliefs and thoughts have been identified, they can be written down and referenced as often as necessary until they become automatic thoughts.

The ABCDE Model of coaching is a great tool that HR managers can use in the workplace to assist developing higher emotional intelligence level in employees. As a result of systematic CBC conferences, employees experiencing instances of low emotional intelligence can be led to have healthy automatic thoughts that will equip them to make wise decisions and produce positive consequences.

Emotional Contagion And Empathy

Emotional contagion in its most positive form is the basis of the human virtue of empathy. We need to be emotionally in tune with others in order to understand them, get along with them and to function effectively in the human social world. Highly sensitive people's finely detailed observational abilities make them more responsive than most to the nuances of other people's feelings. This sometimes leads them to shy away from crowds since the mass of emotional messages is just too confusing. But even one-on-one relating can be emotionally challenging to a person who reads and responds strongly other's subtle emotional cues. Since HSP's own emotional responses are intense, quick to arise and hard to shake off, they often find themselves getting caught up uncomfortably in other people's feelings. Being attuned to the rawness of other people's emotions and even taking them on through emotional contagion can be an unpleasant and aversive experience.

Danger Of Co-Dependency

Since vicariously experiencing others unhappiness, rage or despair are so painful for a highly sensitive individual, it is easy to understand why it would be tempting for them to collude or manage social situations so as to keep others on an emotionally even keel. When the need to ensure that those around them are never angry or upset becomes a preoccupation there is a danger of developing co-dependent relationships.

MASTERY OF EMOTION: A KEY TO A BETTER LIFE

To live a better and happier life, you must take charge of the natural instinctive state of your mind arising from circumstances, moods or relationships with others. Controlling your emotions doesn't mean ignoring them, it means you recognize and take rightful actions on them. You must be in-charge of your emotions day-to-day! If you truly desire unlimited happiness, you must control your emotions. Do you struggle to control your emotions? You have the power to create your state of blissful and favorable emotional circumstances. A clear mind is better and able to control emotions. Un-clutter your mind!

Emotion is the generic term for subjective or conscious experience that is characterized by psycho-physiological expressions, biological reactions and mental states. It is often associated and considered reciprocally influential with temperament, personality, mood, motivation and depression. Emotions can be influenced by hormones and alcohol. It is the force behind human actions and reactions. Emotions can be expressed in the form of fear, joy, envy, excitement, distrust, depression, curiosity, contentment, desire, despair, embarrassment, confidence, gratitude, happiness, shame and shock.

With the harsh weather conditions, the economy in a miserable state, lack of job security, infidel partner, stubborn children, nagging co-workers, and unrest in the society, it can be easy to allow your emotions to run amok. An uncontrolled state of mind can make a bad situation worse. Every emotion begins with a thought. If you learn to control your mind and thoughts, you can rule your emotions. Guard your heart because out of it flows the issues of life. As you think in your heart, so you are. While it does take practice, you can be in firm control of any of the particular feelings that characterize the state of your mind, such as hate, horror, anger, fear, happiness or love.

Learning to control your emotions during challenging times of emotional stress is beneficial to your mental and general health. Emotions play a great role in life, and decisions are often based on feelings. However, problems occur when emotions are out of control. Becoming a master of emotional intelligence which involves emotional literacy, emotional coping and emotional awareness will help improve your emotional sagacity which helps you develop a good emotional freedom technique. To go higher in your career, build good relationships with people and be successful in life, you must keep a tab on your emotional quotient. It is common in day-to-day life to regret those actions we took because of uncontrolled emotion. There are keys that will help you lead a healthy and better emotional state in life.

1. Recognize Your Emotions

Human feelings are expressed in different forms. Take time to understand the nature of your feelings. Some of the most difficult emotions include anger, depression, anxiety and fear; the good News is that they can be subdued.

2. Meditation

The best way to maintain a good emotional health is to focus and dwell on uplifting and empowering thoughts. This will help you harmonize your mind, spirit and body. Meditation helps you to be in-charge of your physical, mental and emotional health. Some people meditate using prayer, yoga, reading a life-enriching book or listening to soul-uplifting music.

3. Affirmation

Affirmation is like confirmation. Through this means you speak faith into your circumstances and gladly expect the best result with cheerful expectancy. Say to yourself, "Am a success." "Am favored beyond measure and things are falling in pleasant places for me." This kind of positive thinking and confessions can change your mood from bad to good.

Over 80% of the things we worry about never happen and 15% out of the other 20% of the time, things don't happen as bad as we thought. Worrying only saps you of energy and vitality. These keys listed above can help you develop your cope capacity, create and be in-charge of your favorable emotional state 24/7. You can handle situations more than you ever thought possible by taking full control of your emotion in your day-to-day life.

GROWING EMOTIONAL INTELLIGENCE

So, what can you do about this? How can you turn this around and begin to grow your Emotional Intelligence?

A first step is to pay more attention to your emotions by noticing their sensations in your body. Before reaching for the TV remote, that sugary snack, caffeine, alcohol, or painkillers, notice the sensations of emotion.

Ask yourself, "If this feeling were located somewhere in my body where that would be?" Then, describe it as a physical sensation. Is it hot, cold? Is there tightness or pressure? Numbness? Tingling? Itching? Nausea? Expansion? Contraction? Rising? Sinking?

While noticing these sensations, especially if they feel uncomfortable, may seem like an odd thing to do to be happier, it's a first step toward connecting with emotional guidance. There's a deeper wisdom nudging you in these sensations. Paying attention to the sensations of emotions is a way to access them, observe them, and allow them to inform you.

Once you are in touch with the sensation, ask yourself, "What is the message in this emotion?" Just notice what comes to mind.

If you're hesitant to engage with emotions, it's important to keep in mind that emotions are transient. No feeling lasts forever. They arise with a purpose. While present, an emotion gives you information about what is going on inside you, around you, and with others-along with energy to do something about it. Once emotional guidance is heeded, it subsides.

How Does Emotional Intelligence Affect Your Life?

Performance at work - EQ helps you to comfortably handle social complexities of workplace, motivate and guide others and succeed in your career. Now-a-days companies view emotional intelligence as being an important aspect and perform EQ testing before hiring.

Physical well-being - Stress is imminent in today's world no matter which profession you belong to. Stress is a familiar factor leading to serious health issues in most of the people. Uncontrolled stress level is known to increase the risk of heart disease. Our immune system suffers when stress level are high.

Mental well-being - Stress affects mental health negatively. You might have read or heard about stressed people going to the extent of committing suicide. When you cannot manage your emotions you become a victim of mood swings or other mental disorders that can seldom allow you to form or maintain strong relationships in life.

Personal relationships - Understanding your emotions help you to express your feelings to your loved ones. When there is a block in communication your relationships suffer both at work and in your personal life.

Improving Communication

If you want to improve your communication skills, it may be easier than you think! It is generally accepted that communication is the skill of both talking and listening, however, there are other more subtle ways to communicate, which can sometimes let us down. Body language and non-verbal cues such as facial expressions and hand gestures all have their place in good communications.

Most people who want to improve their communication skills do so because of their perception of themselves. They may be shy at parties, unwilling to participate in meetings, or feel they have nothing to say at social gatherings.

Yet those same people can often talk the hind legs off a donkey if they are able to discuss a subject close to them - better still if they are in their own home. This all comes down to confidence.

The simplest way to develop the confidence to talk freely at a social event is to pursue a popular pastime, sport or hobby that involves other people. While stamp collecting is fine, unless you happen to be in the same room at the same time as a fellow enthusiast, you'll struggle to make an impression. However, if you opt for let's say, learning a musical instrument, or playing any sport, you will be able to engage people's interest even if you're playing the guitar and they're playing piano. So making good conversation is not necessarily about having the same passions as everybody else - you just have to have a passion for something.

Being a good communicator can also help advance your working career. If you walk into the boss's office staring at your shoes, and mumbling about the pay rise that you deserve, you won't get far. However, if you enter the office with your head held high and your shoulders back, speaking clearly and decisively, you may actually walk out with a bigger raise than you were hoping to achieve.

Changing Negative Emotions

Negativity exists in our lives. There is no way around it. No matter how hard you try to live in the moment, focus on positivity, or practice being grateful every day, you will still experience times of negative emotions in your life. But this can be a good thing. Negative emotions signal that you need to make a change in your life. Whether it is stress, anger, fear, jealously, resentment, or any other negative emotion, the point of them all is to warn you that something needs to change.

Negative Emotions Are Our Number And To Transfer Negative Emotion We Need To :

1.) Change your energy field. Close your eyes and imagine the emotion as energy around you. What does it look like, what color, shape, form etc. does it take? Now allow it to change and smooth out, becoming transformed, harmonized, peaceful. What does it look and feel like now?

2.) Change your perspective on the situation. Reframe it in a way that's positive/productive for you. Ask yourself, how this situation can help you. What is good about it? How are you growing from it? A positive attitude about something can help resolve it for you, even if it's a difficult situation. A new mindset can change everything.

3.) Ask self what the lesson you are learning from this situation is. Knowing the lesson helps transform the negative feeling and take on the mastery of the lesson you are in the process of learning.

4.) Put a new and positive picture in your mind about the situation that is causing the hurtful emotion. Instead of dwelling on the painful scenario or the trauma incident or being yelled at or treated disrespectfully, replace it with one of yourself healed, happy, successful, determined to move on etc. Whatever feels great and counters the old feeling. Keep the new picture in place whenever the old feeling comes up. The mind and body respond quickly to pictures, so this will shift you fast.

5.) Inner Listening. Get very quiet and go into the silence within. Allow your inner guide to bring you new insights, wisdom and solutions for healing and transformation.

6.) Forgiveness means letting go. It doesn't condone bad behavior, but lets the pain go. You and others have the right to make mistakes and grow. Forgive self if needed and forgive others. This doesn't mean that you will choose to stay connected with anyone who harms you. It means you let go of the painful movie, get the lesson and move forward. You stop the images and negative emotions from their endless control over you. Restore your self- esteem if you've acted poorly and wish the other person well if they have. To clean yourself completely, do a systematic of forgiveness for everyone in your life. You will be rejuvenated. Forgive; let go and say goodbye to these emotions.

7.) Change a gripe to a goal. If you regularly complain and feel negatively about something or someone, set a goal for yourself and be determined to accomplish it. For example, if you are jealous of someone who has a degree in art; stop it and find a way to get one for yourself. If you are short of money and angry at others who have it, stop it and chart your path, make a plan to increase your income. Things happen first in the mind, so begin to visualize yourself having what you want already now. Feel the joy of it and for 5 minutes several times a day, sit quietly and feel the emotions you would have if it were yours now. Soon you begin to believe you have it. In the Biology of belief, Bruce Lipton offers scientific proof that we get what we believe.

8.) Thoughts and emotions are intimately connected in fact, inseparable. One leads to the other. What repetitive thoughts do you have that are hurting you? Are you taking charge of your negative thoughts and transforming them? Think the opposite of your negative thought as soon as you catch yourself having it. Correct yourself on a daily basis; over and over. Repetition of the new corrected thought forges a new brain pathway and pattern. Strong intention and follow through is necessary.

Don't let your mind wander all day without direction or self-monitoring. You can change your mind at any moment into a more positive state. Letting your thoughts run wild will take away your peace. Take charge of yourself and choose thoughts that will help you.

9.) What belief about yourself do you want to change

Finances, relationships, self-concept, accomplishment of a specific goal; health, personal qualities etc. Beliefs that limit and cause pain keep your emotions at a painful level, and only you can change that.

Taking Positive New Action

1) Set clear boundaries. You decide what you will and won't accept from people and act on it.

2) Practice assertive communication with others. Tell them how you feel without blame or judgment; just how you feel. Stand up for self if needed.

3) Be creative. Create something positive from your experience.

For example, women who have been abused have set up women's shelters around the country. People who grew up hungry have started programs to feed poor children.

All of these techniques work. Practice and practice and you will see yourself and your life become fulfilled and beautiful. Be very patient with yourself, as this is hard work and takes a lot of self- control, intention and discipline. It's a progressive unfolding of the highest part of self. Over time we blossom!

Steps in Review:

1.) Stop and control self.

2.) Release the emotion.

3.) Transform the emotion.

4.) Take positive new action.

5.) Replace negative emotional reactions with spiritual actions and personal spiritual qualities.

Change your life by taking control of your emotions instead of being taken over by them and held in their grip.

Acknowledge That the Negativity Is A Sign

The first thing you need to do is actually sit down and acknowledge that you are in a negative space. Maybe you've just been dumped and are feeling sad, or maybe you are stressed out and resenting your job. It is OK to feel this way. In fact, it's normal!

Sometimes bad things happen that impact our lives in negative ways. The oft-used phrase "shit happens" nails it on the head. Shit really does happen, and it is fine to experience some negative emotions when it does. The important part is what you choose to do next. Once you have accepted your negative emotions you need to acknowledge that they are a sign that something needs to change. Do not ignore them. You are feeling that way for a reason. It is time to make some positive changes!

Figure Out What Action Is Required

Now that you are at one with the idea that some change is required in your life you need to figure out what that actual change is. What are your emotions telling you to do? It's normally pretty obvious. Are you stressed in your job? Find a new one. Hating your relationship? End it. Bored with life? Sell everything and take a holiday. Well it might not be that simple as this but I can assure you that it is pretty simple. You can go a little deeper by assessing exactly what is negative about your current situation. Try to break it down to the smallest possible level.

For example, once you start doing this you might realize that your job really isn't that stressful normally but it is just this one project that is killing you. So now you know that you only need to fix your current workload and you actually don't need to quit your job, sell your things, and go live in a cave as a hermit. Phew.

Take a step

This is the hard part. Acknowledging the negativity and figuring out what action is required is easy most of the time. Actually doing something about it is where most people will encounter trouble. The biggest blocker to taking action is a fear of change. People are often scared of change because they do not know exactly what is going to happen once the change occurs. Well I've got news for you - the future is constantly changing and you will never ever know exactly what is going to happen. Never!

The very definition of the future means that it a step forward in time which means that things have changed. Time has progressed and billions of actions have taken place. And this occurs every second! You cannot stop the change process because but you can make sure that in your life you are the one in control of the changes. Inaction and indecision are common symptoms of a fear of change (and fear of failure/success). By not taking action you let everyone else in the world decide what will happen for your life. You give away your power and become helpless. But if you choose to be decisive and start taking action you begin creating the changes that you want instead of being inundated by the changes that everyone else wants.

Keep Adjusting

You won't get it right first time but you will learn a hell of a lot along the way. Maybe the first change you made was not enough. Maybe you really did hate your job after all and just fixing that one project didn't help.

So you readjust. You take stock again, assess the situation, and make another change. Another positive change that is. Or maybe the first change you made was too drastic and you realize that the original situation was better than the one you are in now. That's fine too. Just readjust and try again until you get it right and find a place where you feel happy, excited, and passionate.

Delete Negating Emotions From Your System

There is nothing beautiful about negative emotions; it's an obstacle to living a well-deserved life. despite the fact that life doesn't always turn out the way we expect we must keep a check on our emotions and not allow circumstances decide how we live our life .Negative emotions, across the board, could be reduced and the cumulative effects of the emotions from all spiritual experiences could be deleted-just like you delete things from a computer's hard drive. Essentially, we would then have less negative emotion to ruin us. And when we have one new emotion, it would not trigger all the previous old emotions in combination with each other.

In the case of a mother, for example, worrying about her child's welfare is not going to change anything for the better. In fact, the mother worrying about the child's health will actually make the condition worse for the child, so the worries have to be reduced or pretty much deleted. There should be no worries, no negative thoughts and no negative emotions about a child.

It's not about suppressing, repressing or denying the negative emotions and negative thoughts. Nor does it work to numb yourself out or try to forget about them. These emotions and thoughts should be truthfully deleted, so they can't come back and haunt the situation. If left undeleted, negative emotions can cause a continuous struggle throughout your entire life-not only your life, but the lives of those around you.

You can learn the skill needed to delete emotions for yourself and others. In order to delete the emotion of sadness, for example, you could just get in touch with one thing in your life that makes you feel the emotion of sadness. This establishes a baseline that you can check into later in order to feel the change.

Essentially, all you do is put some thought energy on your midline while deleting the cumulative effect of all the sadness in your spiritual experiences. There is a three stage deletion process to this protocol, but after you experience the process, it would become more automatic and almost instantaneous. This is a good skill to learn for everyone.

CONCLUSION

Paying attention to your emotion is the first step to becoming a master of emotional intelligence, emotions are inborn and we have seen through the course of this book that emotions can be found in humans as well as in animals in the form of empathy, we see that animals are able to relate with their owners during times of distress, pain sorry, fear we see that some behaviors like adaptability allows an individual to understand the emotions or motives of others and as a result they are more willing to adapt to a situation than a person who can only understand what they personally are feeling. We come to realize that empathy is the highest level of communication skill and it should be put to use more often as it allows one to relate well with peoples unspoken words and the feelings created by them in others. Empathy is also responsible for how we respond to other's feelings sympathetically so that they can win their trust, which promotes communication further. Our fear of failure, anger, and frustration suddenly drop away, allowing for a more meaningful dialogue and a deepening of relationships, we are finally able to feel what others feel and skills like emotional control helps the individual control their emotions when they try to go overboard . During times of stress emotional intelligence plays a great role as they are able to find a way around it, they are optimistic and are good at building strong relationships. We also learnt that being a good communicator can also help advance your working career, improve relationship between employee and boss; EI and EQ are useful for human relations as they help clients decide

Developing these skills takes a lot of time, even years. But a little conscious effort can reduce this time down to a fraction of how long it would ordinarily take. The journey to mastering emotional intelligence is not for individuals who are ready to make a difference in life and make things work out for them as they climb up the ladder of success. You can Change your life by taking charge of your emotions rather of being taken over by them and held in their grip. One must remember that emotions are powerful but we decide what gets to us. Mastery will be within our reach once we are able to acknowledge the benefits of emotional intelligence to our lives. Remember to acknowledge That Negativity Is A Sign , then try to figure Out What Action Is Required to make this problem go away , then take the necessary actions.

www.ingramcontent.com/pod-product-compliance
Lightning Source LLC
Chambersburg PA
CBHW070905080526
44589CB00013B/1183